"In *Free of Me*, Sharon exposes a mind-set that is not only widespread but prevents many of us from experiencing true freedom in Christ: living for self. Drawing on her own journey, Sharon offers deep spiritual wisdom through relatable stories to reveal the peril of self-focus, and she invites readers into a bigger, better story. In a culture captivated by self, this book is a must-read."

Christine Caine, founder of A21 and Propel Women

"*Free of Me* may be one of the most important truths for our times. This is not a book to only read—this is a book to become. Sharon Hodde Miller hands every woman a key with these pages that no woman can afford to pass up. *Free of Me* is the breaking free every soul desperately seeks."

Ann Voskamp, author of *New York Times* bestsellers *The Broken Way* and *One Thousand Gifts*

"Sharon spotlights the crippling disease of self-focus and shows us how to break free from its entanglements. If you want to walk in God's life-giving truth, this book will help you do just that!"

Lysa TerKeurst, *New York Times* bestselling author; president of Proverbs 31 Ministries

"The most deceptive lies the enemy tells us concern how we see ourselves. *Free of Me* teaches us to see ourselves as God sees us. It is honest, down-to-earth, biblical, faithful, and gospel rich. Sharon writes like she lives—authentically, carefully, and accessibly. I count her a great friend and this a great book."

J. D. Greear, pastor, The Summit Church; author of *Stop Asking Jesus Into Your Heart: How to Know for Sure You Are Saved*

"Sharon's passion in life is Jesus and giving him away to others. Sharon has lived intentionally and her perspective is hard-fought in the trenches of following Jesus and conforming her life to look like his. She is a thoughtful, contagious force—so prepare to love Jesus more."

Jennie Allen, founder of IF:Gathering;
author of *Nothing to Prove*

"There is a troubling trend in Christian messages today: gospels which are more about self than Christ. In *Free of Me*, Sharon takes aim at this false gospel, revealing its emptiness and why it can't deliver. Through personal testimony and scriptural backing, she explains how we can reject these messages and focus on the one true gospel that frees. In these pages, Sharon issues a bold call we all need to hear, which is why I highly recommend this book."

Ed Stetzer, Billy Graham Distinguished Chair, Wheaton College

"One of the best things for a healthy marriage, workplace, parent situation, or any calling is to realize the world is not orbiting around our axis. True joy is found when we realize there is a bigger story to tell, and the tyranny of 'me' is actually a terrible slave driver. In *Free of Me*, Sharon paints this picture more beautifully than anyone I know. I hope you are encouraged as much as I was."

Jefferson Bethke, author of *Love That Lasts*

"Too many books written by and for Christian women are shallow and trivial. This is not one of them. *Free of Me* provides deep biblical and human understanding and offers the best sort of wisdom: honest, hard-won, and biblically sound. I will be recommending this book widely and enthusiastically to many for years to come."

Karen Swallow Prior, PhD, professor of English at Liberty University; author of *Booked: Literature in the Soul of Me* and *Fierce Convictions—The Extraordinary Life of Hannah More: Poet, Reformer Abolitionist*

"Rarely do I read a book with the powerful combination of eloquence and practical truth, but *Free of Me* has it. Sharon Miller has woven honest personal stories with steady wisdom in guiding us to the joy that comes from a life of freedom from self. What a gift to our *me first* culture. This book is a sweet discipling on every page. I'm grateful for the message of *Free of Me* and the lives it will truly set free."

Lisa Whittle, speaker; author of
I Want God and *Put Your Warrior Boots On*

"Determined to recover joy she had known and somehow lost, Sharon Hodde Miller set out on a quest to find the root of soul-sapping insecurity that was sabotaging relationships and roles she once loved. What she discovered is deeper than self-help; it is soul healing and life-shifting. In *Free of Me*, Sharon takes us with her on a gut-honest search for answers to the questions our hearts are asking: *What's wrong with me? Why do I feel like I'm never enough?* Grounded in God's Word and packed with personal stories, insightful revelations, applicable resolutions, and sometimes humorous yet convicting truth, this message will set you free!"

Renee Swope, bestselling author of *A Confident Heart*

"In this honest, engaging, and refreshing book, Sharon adjusts our gaze ever so slightly, but that slight perspective shift makes all the difference. The struggle against chronic self-focus is personal to me, and I'm grateful to Sharon for this manual of sorts to help redirect my gaze back to the gospel, to others, to God."

Amanda Bible Williams, author and chief
content officer at She Reads Truth

Free of Me

Free of Me

Why Life Is Better When It's
NOT ABOUT YOU

SHARON HODDE MILLER

BakerBooks

a division of Baker Publishing Group
Grand Rapids, Michigan

© 2017 by Sharon Hodde Miller

Published by Baker Books
a division of Baker Publishing Group
PO Box 6287, Grand Rapids, MI 49516-6287
www.bakerbooks.com

Printed in the United States of America

Library of Congress Cataloging-in-Publication Data
Names: Miller, Sharon Hodde, 1981– author.
Title: Free of me : why life is better when it's not about you / Sharon Hodde Miller.
Description: Grand Rapids, MI : Baker Books, a division of Baker Publishing
    Group, [2017] | Includes bibliographical references.
Identifiers: LCCN 2017025098 | ISBN 9780801075230 (pbk.)
Subjects: LCSH: Theological anthropology—Christianity. | Self—Religious
    aspects—Christianity. | Self-perception—Religious aspects—Christianity. |
    Liberty—Religious aspects—Christianity.
Classification: LCC BT701.3 .M57 2017 | DDC 248.4—dc23
LC record available at https://lccn.loc.gov/2017025098

Author is represented by The Christopher Ferebee Agency, www.christopherferebee.com.

18   19   20   21   22   23   7   6   5   4   3

To my three great joys, Ike, Isaac, and Coen.
Loving you is God's kindness to me.

Contents

PART THREE: HOW TO BE FREE OF ME

Introduction

*I*t's not about you."

These are the famous opening words to Rick Warren's bestselling book *The Purpose Driven Life*, and when I began telling people about the vision for this book, these were the words I returned to. I didn't land on them intentionally, but organically, because they capture my own journey well. I couldn't ignore the way people's ears perked up when they heard the phrase. Something resonated, as if it was a message they needed.

Even so, I wondered if the phrase was too bold. "It's not about you" can sound scolding, which is not the message I intended. I consulted my friend Karen, a fellow writer and wise woman of God, to see what she thought of the phrase. "Is it too *in your face?*" I asked. "Do you think it has a place? Do Christians have the ears to hear it?"

"I love it!" she declared without hesitation. "I think this message offers something needed, that people *want* to hear."

What Karen understood, and what God has taught me over the years, is that there are two ways of saying, "It's not about you." One is a rebuke, a finger-wagging sentiment, usually directed at "young people these days." But there is another way of saying it, and hearing it too: "It's not about you" can be freedom. The friend who rejected you, the parent who hurt you, the boss who insulted you, the neighbor who was rude to you—*it's not about you*. Their brokenness, their temper, their cold, piercing words; none of that was about you, but them. When your house isn't as big as you'd like it to be, or your ministry isn't as successful, or your name isn't as well known, thank goodness *it's not about you*. Your marriage, your calling, your life here on earth, none of it is about you. It's all about God, from the first to the last, and that is some of the best news on earth.

When you make things about you that are not about you, it's a terrible burden. Living for yourself is a crushing weight. Deep down, we all know that if we could stop trying to people-please, stop trying to measure up, stop focusing on our flaws, and stop dwelling on rejection, life would be a lot easier. If we could only focus a little less on ourselves and a little more on God, our shoulders would feel so much lighter.

I think we all know that. But the challenge is, how?

The Allure of Self

Over two thousand years ago, the Roman poet Ovid penned a cautionary tale about vanity. At the center of it was a man named Narcissus, whose appearance was stunningly handsome. This man was not just quarterback handsome, not even supermodel handsome. Narcissus was sublimely intoxicating to everyone, including himself. His face was so beautiful that, after glimpsing his reflection in a spring, Narcissus fell in love with himself.

Narcissus was captivated by his own reflection, to the point that he couldn't bear to leave it. He refused to part with his watery gaze, so he remained there, enchanted by what he saw. Hours turned into days, and days into weeks, and his body decayed into a shell, until one afternoon, Narcissus laid down beside his reflection and died.

In the age of social media, it's amazing how relevant this ancient story remains. It still has so many lessons for our contemporary moment, the first being that **vanity isn't new.** Vanity did not arrive with smartphones or selfies, but is as old as humankind.

This story also points to the **allure of self,** and how irresistible it can be. Notice that Narcissus didn't simply like what he saw but was wholly and completely consumed by it. He could not pry his gaze away from himself, and that is the human condition. All of us struggle with the pull of self-focus, whether we recognize the temptation or not. Even when we do recognize it, the habit is hard to break, because self-image is constantly enticing.

Another timeless truth tucked into this story is the **peril of self.** Narcissus's vanity kept him from living his life, and self-focus does the same to us. It results in a slow but steady spiritual death, often without us even noticing. Self-focus hurts our relationships, shrinks our faith, kills our confidence, and ultimately steals all our joy. When it creeps into our families, our friendships, and our work, it turns the beautiful into the burdensome.

That was my story. Self-focus robbed me of my joy. It affected my marriage, my calling, and even my relationship with God. I was so focused on my own image and reputation that I began to wither inside.

And just like Narcissus, I couldn't stop looking.

The Vision of This Book

Shifting your focus off of yourself and onto God is much harder than it sounds. As broken people, our gaze naturally drifts inward, making vanity a tough pattern to shake, and that is why I wrote this book. Once I was able to see my own self-preoccupation—both the allure and the peril of it—God took me on a long journey to freedom. He taught me how to adjust my sight back onto him, and it literally changed my life. Once I grasped the truth that life is not about me and shifted my focus onto Christ, it became the song of my heart, one I can't stop singing to others.

In the pages that follow, I have done my best to communicate the vision God gave me, because I want it to capture you the way it captured me. You will read about my own story of self-focus, as well as the pain it caused in seven areas of my life. You will also learn four practical steps out of the trap of self-focus. Not a single page comes from a place of judgment, but from the grit of having lived it myself.

Every chapter includes a "Discussion Questions" section, because I hope you will read this book in community. God designed the whole Christian life to be walked out in the context of a "people," and I can't think of a better way to combat self-focus than by linking arms with others. Find a friend (or three!) who is committed to honesty, grace, and growth, and embark on this journey together. At the end of each chapter you will also find a "Focus Verse" and a "Focus Prayer," designed to shift your gaze away from self and onto God. The transformation described in this book is not possible without the help of the Holy Spirit, so I hope these prayers remind you of his role, as well as release you from the burden of achieving this vision on your own.

Finally, I want you to know that if you are reading these words, I have prayed for you. On countless mornings, I woke up thinking of you, burdened for your own self-made captivities. I asked God to shine on the hidden places in your heart and grant you the courage to see yourself honestly, because this book asks you to do something hard: to look straight in the face of your vanity. It's uncomfortable and it's humbling, but it's how we break the spell of self. And oh how it is worth it! I pray, so desperately, that it changes your life the way that it has changed mine. I pray you will be set free of *me*.

PART 1

Self-Distracted

one

Mirror Girl

Are you looking for accolades? Are you looking for applause? Are you looking for approval? Are you looking for acceptance? Because that stuff will kill you. The Devil will make sure you get all of that. Especially early, and especially young, so that you then collapse when you're unapplauded, when you're unapproved, when you're unaccepted, and when you're unwanted.[1]

—Christine Caine

This is my story.

"I may be little, but I'm smart!"

According to my parents, I made this pronouncement at the age of six. I was a tiny twig of a kid, always in the zero percentile of the pediatrician's chart, smaller than everyone my age. Because of my size, I was an easy target for teasing. There was the boy who always called me "shrimp" and my entire sixth-grade math class who used to take turns wrapping their hands—fingertip to fingertip—around my ankle. I was carnival-attraction small, but it didn't bother me. I was confident and tough. I knew I could hold my own.

As I got older, I transitioned into my clumsy middle school years, but my confidence soldiered on. In fact, it escorted me all the way through high school, in spite of a deep and abiding awkward phase. To this day, my confidence still surprises me, because I was *factually* more awkward than my peers. I know everyone says that about themselves, but it's true. Take my hair. Until my freshman year of high school, my haircut was one snip away from a mullet—long in the back, with bangs wrapping around my forehead like a bowl. My bangs extended so far behind my ears that my friends referred to them as my "360 bangs": from the front, they had the illusion of encircling my entire head. From the side, I was early '90s Billy Ray.

Unlike some middle school girls whose disaster haircuts were carefully crafted, mine was haphazard. I never thought about my hair. I got my hair cut at a local barbershop where the clientele was 99 percent male, and I never even noticed. I never thought, *Hmm, everyone here is a middle-aged man. Maybe I shouldn't get my hair cut here.* Not even on my radar.

Then there were my teeth. My teeth required extensive orthodontic work, which included headgear and an expander on the roof of my mouth. My mouth looked like I had gotten in a fight with a chain-link fence.

My outfits were more typical middle school fare. Each month I combed through the pages of *Teen* magazine, hoping to recreate the images inside. This was decades before Pinterest, but my outfits were the '90s equivalents of Pinterest fails. In the days of grunge, I wore yellow construction worker boots on skinny stick legs, which gave me the appearance of a miniature Frankenstein.

That was me. I was not the cutest. And in case you think I'm exaggerating, I have a testimony! At sixteen years old I began to emerge from my awkward phase. The braces were off and the 360 bangs had grown out. I was starting to look like an actual human girl. Then one afternoon, I was serving punch at a family gathering. An old family friend walked over to say hello. Her daughter was my age, and we'd grown up together.

"Sharon, you look gorgeous!" she crowed. "You have blossomed into *such* a beautiful young woman."

I blushed, but it did feel nice. I wasn't used to people complimenting my appearance. Then she kept going.

"I remember when you used to come over to play at my house, and I would think, 'Sharon is such a sweet girl. I hope she grows out of this.' AND YOU DID!"

This is as close as it gets to someone telling you, point-blank, that you were an ugly kid.

That's why my self-esteem was surprising. By the world's standard of beauty, I fell pretty far short, but my confidence never wavered. I was focused on school and friends and doing things that I loved. I was secure.

A Fragile Confidence

My confidence continued throughout high school and most of college. It wasn't until I graduated and wasn't an *instant* success that my self-esteem began to flag. I took a job where I was on the bottom rung of the ladder, and it made me feel small and unimportant. My pride thrashed against the obscurity of my work, while my self-esteem swayed between entitlement and self-doubt. I was used to being the leader, not the copy machine operator. *This can't be right, right?*

It was also during that season that I began and ended a series of dating relationships, and every breakup felt like a personal failure. Added to those heartbreaks were a number of friendship breakdowns, which deflated my confidence more. For the first time in my life, I wasn't succeeding, and it initiated a seismic shift in my identity. Until then, insecurity was an occasional visitor in my life; soon it was a steady companion.

However, the knockout punch to my self-esteem was yet to come. A year after my husband and I were married, we moved from our home state of North Carolina to Chicago, leaving behind an extensive network of friends. I had relied on them heavily, so I was anxious to make new friends in Illinois. But as the months dragged on, a friend group didn't materialize. I made a friend here and there, but then one would move away, or our life stages made it difficult to connect. It wasn't long before I began to feel isolated and alone.

About the same time, I was writing more and my blog was steadily growing. I enjoyed writing and felt fulfilled by it, but I also began to meet writers who were much more successful than I was. They had massive ministries and huge followings, and compared to them my blog looked like a hobby. Over time, the comparison began to crush me. I felt haunted by my own invisibility. The combination of loneliness and obscurity was the one-two punch that crumpled my confidence altogether.

Somewhere between childhood and adulthood, my confidence left me. For a long time, I wondered why. What happened to that "small but smart" little girl?

Eventually I decided to find out, which meant looking back on those early years through a different lens.

A Nice Christian Girl

I have always had a great relationship with my parents. I never went through an angsty phase when I hated my mom and dad or was embarrassed by them. I believed them, I trusted them, and I seldom pushed back. I also lived to please them.

In fact, I lived to please most of the adults in my life: teachers, coaches, pastors, parents of my friends. I was a "good kid" and I relished that reputation. I also made good grades, and I was proud of that fact.

My track record was so pristine that I still remember the handful of times I was in trouble at school. Once in kindergarten I was talking to my "boyfriend" when I was supposed to be listening to the teacher. It was the only day I didn't earn a smiley face sticker. In eighth grade I accidentally discussed a test within earshot of a student who had not taken it. It was an innocent mistake, but my teacher threatened to send me to the Honor Council. She eventually dropped the charge, but the shame was mortifying.

Those were the two great "scandals" of my childhood. Otherwise, I ran my life on the straight and narrow. I loved that my teachers loved me. I loved that my parents trusted me. I was a nice Christian girl, and the world was a friendly place to kids like me.

That said, there is a special temptation facing nice Christian kids. Although my confidence did not stand on my appearance, it stood on something equally flimsy, which was a deep-seated need for affirmation. Because I was such a good kid, I received a lot of praise, and soon that became my identity. I *needed* the praise, which meant the line between doing good for goodness' sake and doing good for appearance's sake became increasingly blurry. After a while, I wasn't sure if I was nice to people because it was Christlike or because I so needed the acclaim. Maybe it was both.

The truth is, I needed to be liked in order to feel good about myself. My identity was bound up in the opinions of others, and I craved affirmation. As a result, I evolved into a serial people-pleaser.

People-pleasing is a funny thing, because it seems "others-focused," but it's not about others at all. It's about you. You want other people to think well of *you*. You want people to say nice things about *you*. You help and you do favors and you struggle to say no because you don't want people to be mad at *you*. Yes, your self-confidence hinges on the well-being of others, but at the end of the day people-pleasing is really in service to yourself.

For many Christians, our niceness isn't about witnessing to Jesus but getting people to like us. That's why kindness, not niceness, is a fruit of the Spirit. That's also why the prophets are never described as being "nice." Speaking truth and living courageously means people won't always think you are nice. God and "nice" are two allegiances that often compete.

By nurturing the nice Christian girl image, I was nurturing a focus on myself. I was concerned with maintaining *my* image and *my* reputation, while priding myself on how thoughtful, well-liked, and selfless I was. I was blind to the gradual drift in my focus, because my idea of a self-centered person was narrow. I thought self-centered people were selfish, mean, and oblivious to the needs of others, but those weren't really my vices. My self-centeredness didn't prevent me from caring for my neighbor, because my self-centeredness *required* it. I needed to be accepted! I needed to be liked! I needed to be thought well of! Being nice to people was a surefire way to have all those things.

That is how subtle self-focus can be. It doesn't always look like a devil with horns. It's gradual and quiet and it creeps in on the back of good intentions. I wanted to be a good person, and I wanted to be liked, and that desire became idolatry of self. I lived to serve my reputation, and as long as people liked me, I felt great about myself.

Throughout my entire childhood, I had based my confidence on people's approval, applause, and acceptance, and I had lots of it. The system worked really well for me.

Until it didn't.

The Mirror Reflex

It's hard not to look in a mirror, isn't it? Try walking by a mirror, or any reflective surface, without checking yourself out. I am terrible about this. When I was in college, I was eating lunch with an older woman from church. She was a mentor to numerous women my age, and we sat across from one another chatting while we ate. Out of nowhere she interrupted herself and asked, "Is there a mirror behind me? You keep looking past me."

She craned her neck around and, sure enough, there it was. A mirror. I had been looking at myself the entire meal.

This story still embarrasses me to think about, but it's also a common behavior. Looking at your reflection is practically a human reflex. If you walk by a mirror you are *going to* take a look. We all do it.

This reflex is powerful. It's so powerful that we even apply it to relationships. We treat people as if they are a reflection of us and our self-worth. Affirmation and praise give us a positive self-image, while criticism or rejection gives us a negative one.

I call this the "mirror reflex"—the tendency to treat people as a reflection of yourself. For me, the mirror reflex began in the form of people-pleasing, but it became a way of life. Eventually I turned my marriage, friendships, parenting, work, even my relationship with God into mirrors reflecting back on me. When this happens, the "mirror reflex" has two major consequences.

First, **your self-image is shaped by people, possessions, and profession.** You look to these things to determine your self-worth. When the reflection is good, you feel great about yourself. When the reflection is bad, you feel insecure.

Second, **you make everything about you, even when it's not about you.** Maybe a friend doesn't say hi to you at work, so you assume she's upset with you. Maybe the cashier at the store is impolite, and you take it personally. Maybe you volunteer to serve at church and feel hurt when nobody thanks you. When you treat people like mirrors, you create a world that is all about you, and that is what I had done. I had become a self-focused person without even realizing it. I had equated self-centeredness with selfishness, so I didn't recognize the subtler forms of self-centeredness that had crept into my heart.

I'm not alone. Most of us have an idea of what it means to be self-centered, and it's usually "other people out there," like narcissistic reality stars or the jerk who takes two parking spots. We're less attuned to our own self-focus, mostly because it's not as obvious.

Take social media. Studies show that Facebook directly impacts personal satisfaction, because users interpret the "likes" and comments as a measure of their worth. Think about how you feel when a friend receives more "likes" or more comments on her photos than you. It's easy to compare: *Why don't people like my photos as much? Are my kids not as cute? Do people care about me less?* For many people, these comparisons are *about us*, which leaves us feeling small, unimportant, and overlooked.[2] But it doesn't stop with social media. Consider marriage and relationships. Have you ever pressured your spouse into doing something, or acting a certain way, because of how it reflected on you? Has an unhealthy dating relationship shaped the way you see yourself? How about friendships? When a friend didn't call you back or didn't respond to an email, did your imagination run wild with questions like, "What did I do wrong?" Maybe she was simply busy or had a family emergency, but you immediately jumped to conclusions about yourself. That's because all of our relationships can function as mirrors, and as I was beginning to discover, I had constructed an entire world of them.

Trapped by My Reflection

I was Narcissus. I was transfixed by my own reflection and suffering a slow spiritual decay. By making my relationships and my ministry about me, my confidence was bound up in their successes or failures. A successful writing ministry meant I had value. Successful friendships meant I was lovable. But the reverse was also true, which left me devastated and insecure.

This is the natural course of all idolatry. Whenever we put anything before God, it's only a matter of time before it turns on us.

This is even true of self-image. When we live for ourselves—even in an innocent, nice Christian kid kind of way—it's only a matter of time before the idol consumes us.

That was my problem. I existed in a world of mirrors, and by the time I recognized the problem, it was too ingrained for me to snap out of it. I wanted to stop living for myself and my reputation and start living fully for God, but I had to reprogram my heart, and that's easier said than done. As much as I tried, I couldn't take my eyes off myself and place them back on God. I needed help, but it was going to take a while to find it.

Focus Verse

"Search me, God, and know my heart; test me and know my anxious thoughts. See if there is any offensive way in me, and lead me in the way everlasting."—Psalm 139:23–24

Focus Prayer

Father, Son, and Holy Spirit, I cannot know myself honestly apart from you. So I invite you to search me, to know my heart, and to open my eyes to see myself honestly. Awaken me to the broken places I like to ignore and the dark corners I cannot see. Lay claim to them and deal with them, for my good and your glory. Amen.

Discussion Questions

1. Looking back on your life, when were you the most confident in yourself?
2. In which areas of your life have you struggled most with insecurity?

3. Can you pinpoint when those insecurities began to creep in, and why?

4. Can you identify any areas in which you struggle with the mirror reflex?

5. What do you think is the difference between loving yourself and focusing on yourself?

Two

Forgetting Myself

True humility is not thinking less of yourself; it's thinking
of yourself less.[1]

—Rick Warren

*H*ave you ever noticed that affirmation in one area of your
life doesn't always transfer to other areas? My husband
can tell me I'm a great writer, but it doesn't mean much
without the approval of my peers. A father can tell his daughter
she's beautiful, but that's cold comfort in a high school cafeteria.
I can tell my husband he's an amazing pastor, but he also needs
positive feedback at church.

Six months after we moved to Chicago, I found myself in that
place. I missed my friends from home so much I could hardly bear
it. I was tired of putting myself out there, and I didn't have much
to show for it. Finding friends was like dating, and I was the girl
no one wanted to dance with.

I will never forget coming home one afternoon and collapsing into my husband's arms. "What's wrong with me?" I wailed. "I had friends in North Carolina. Why can't I make any here?" I sucked in a gasp of air before moaning on about my loneliness and dissolving into a puddle of mascara. My poor husband was probably sitting there thinking, "What am I, chopped liver? You are not *alone in the world!*" Instead, he put his arms around me and spoke the apology of an understanding man:

"I'm sorry I can't be a group of girls."

I laughed. It was funny because it was true. I had a great husband, but it wasn't the same as having girlfriends. I needed both. Affirmation in one area doesn't compensate for all the rest, even with God. Scripture speaks all kinds of truths over us—we are wonderfully made, we are seen, we are loved—but it isn't always enough. Most of us desire affirmation elsewhere. It's like, *I'm glad you think that, God, but I would still like a boyfriend!* Knowing God loves us does not always produce security in all areas of our lives.

That was how I felt. In addition to having a supportive husband and parents, I knew how much God loved me. I knew what the Bible said about me. I read Christian books about insecurity and blog posts about how special I was. And still, it wasn't enough. I was plagued by self-doubt, and I couldn't figure out why. Why weren't those truths "working"?

Around that time, I returned to a book by Tim Keller called *The Freedom of Self-Forgetfulness*. The term "self-forgetfulness" has a long history in the Christian faith, but it does not mean erasing the memory of your self or living as if your self doesn't exist. The best way to understand this term is to think about your mind-set after a loss. At first, the memory is all-consuming. You can't stop thinking about it. Your brain can never rest, because it always bends back toward the trauma. You cannot stop remembering it.

But over time, the memory loosens its grip. It's no longer the first thing you remember when you wake up in the morning, and no longer with you every hour. There might even come a time when you haven't thought about it in days, or weeks. You will never forget what happened, but you are free from remembering it all the time, and self-forgetfulness is a lot like that. You will never be able to forget yourself entirely, but you can be free from thinking about yourself all the time.[2]

This analogy is also helpful because it reminds us just what kind of "freedom" we are talking about here. From a worldly perspective, freedom usually means independence, the liberty to do whatever you want. From a gospel perspective, "freedom" is freedom from sin and the flesh, not to live however you want but to live for God. Freedom means you are no longer bound by the tyranny of self, but you are free to focus on Christ. It's not about greater independence, but greater dependence on God. That's the kind of freedom we were built for.

I had read Keller's book on self-forgetfulness many times, but that time it finally clicked. Keller had pinpointed the root of my struggle, which is that I had been approaching my insecurities all wrong. As Keller explains, many of the strategies we use to combat insecurity don't work, and there's a reason for that:

> If someone has a problem with low self-esteem we, in our modern world, seem to have only one way of dealing with it. That is remedying it with high self-esteem. We tell someone that they need to see that they are a great person, they need to see how wonderful they are. We tell them to look at all the great things they have accomplished. We tell them they just need to stop worrying about what people say about them. We tell them they need to set their own standards and accomplish them—and then make their own evaluation of themselves.[3]

That's how I had been addressing my own insecurity—with positive self-talk—but Keller says this approach cannot deliver. High self-esteem can't give us the freedom and wholeness our souls crave, because high self-esteem is a mirage. It promises something it does not possess. In fact, the pursuit of it is just a distraction.

Running Distracted

To understand why self-esteem and self-help messages can be distracting, consider this word picture in Hebrews 12:1–2:

> *Let us throw off everything that hinders and the sin that so easily entangles. And let us run with perseverance the race marked out for us, fixing our eyes on Jesus, the pioneer and perfecter of faith.*

Let me begin by admitting I feel ill-equipped to explain this verse, because I am not a runner. Not even a little. My philosophy on running is that I only run when someone is trying to murder me. I know almost nothing about running.

However, I *do* know about walking on treadmills. I have a lot of experience with them, both good and bad. I once fell so hard that everyone in the gym—I mean *everyone*—stopped running and stared, while I lay on the floor like a pile of laundry. I tried to play it off, but my body thudded too loudly on the ground. There was no recovering.

That was not my first treadmill injury, nor is it likely to be my last, but these experiences have taught me two important things: (1) I need to stop walking on treadmills, and (2) I fall when I'm distracted. If I look at my phone or at someone behind me, that's when I stumble. The only way to stay balanced is to remain focused ahead.

Returning to Hebrews 12:1–2, these verses are saying the same thing: your focus matters. Your focus is the difference between hitting the pavement and reaching the finish line. The problem is, many of us are running distracted. We're stumbling through life because our focus is off. It's an easy mistake to make in a me-centered world. When we're dealing with insecurity, brokenness, and fear, the world says, "Focus on YOU! You are great. You are special. You are perfect just the way you are." This message even has a God spin to it: "God has an amazing plan for *you*!"

And you know what? A lot of that is true. Those messages are not bad or wrong in and of themselves. It's important to take care of yourself and give yourself time to heal. I affirm that entirely, and more importantly, so does God.

But. That can't be your focus. *You* cannot be your focus. Otherwise you're running distracted. That's why the promises of high self-esteem—of focusing on yourself, working on yourself, and boosting yourself up—can only take you so far. If your faith exists to make you feel better about yourself, you're going to veer off course. You'll find yourself returning to those messages again and again, never fully moving on, because you're not advancing toward the finish line. You've lost focus.

That's what happened to me. I was stuck, and the only thing that got me back in the race was realizing that my self-esteem wasn't the problem. The problem was my focus. I couldn't enjoy the freedom of living for Christ, because I wasn't living for Christ. I was living for me. My eyes were fixed on *me*.

What I eventually came to realize was this: there are two root causes of insecurity. The first is obvious: *low self-esteem*.[4] Low self-esteem is real and painful, and the gospel has an answer for it. When you struggle with degrading lies about who you are, the answer is biblical truth—about God, and about yourself. His love, his compassion, his acceptance, his affirmation: it's all a healing balm for the wounded.

However, there is a second root cause of insecurity, which is *self-preoccupation*. Self-focus assumes that every slight, every rejection, every awkward interaction *must* be about you. Self-focus raises the stakes of dating, parenting, working, and serving by turning it all into a referendum on your worth. Self-focus also magnifies your flaws, because you are constantly aware of them.

Now, it's not always easy to sort these two causes out. Low self-esteem and self-preoccupation intertwine and overlap, and sometimes one leads to the other, but it is still crucial to know the difference between them. Why? Because they require different solutions. If you try to treat your self-preoccupation the way you treat low self-esteem—namely, with affirmation—it actually makes the problem worse. The affirmation only *feeds* your self-focus and further entrenches the source of your insecurity.

That was my problem. That was why self-help messages weren't helping me. What I needed was not high self-esteem. What I needed was self-forgetfulness. That's also the reason affirmation in one area of your life doesn't always translate into others: it's not addressing the real problem. Many times, the real problem is an unhealthy focus on yourself, and its need for affirmation is insatiable. One or two people isn't enough. God himself is not enough. Self-focus needs *all the people* to like you all the time.

The only path out of self-focus is self-forgetfulness, which is why Christian messages about "believing in myself" weren't helping me. Instead of solving the problem, they were contributing to it. Rather than pry my gaze off of myself, they simply handed me a mirror with a Jesus tint. What I needed was freedom from thinking about myself, even when the thinking about myself was positive.

Again, I want to emphasize how important it is to take care of yourself. It is *essential* to know God's truth about you! If you have been hurt, abused, or lied to, you need time and space to heal. Soak in those truths. Embrace God's love. Don't push yourself to get back in the race.

But know this: while those truths are helpful, they are also limited in their helpfulness. The answers to life's greatest questions are not inside you or even about you. Whether it's the solution to your deepest needs or the healing to your biggest wounds, your self does not have them. At some point, you've got to turn your attention to the One who does, to fix your eyes on the only One who can heal your wounds and set you free.

At some point, you have to look out.

Does that mean you should neglect or ignore yourself completely? Not at all. The best runners take care of their bodies. An injured foot needs attention and time to heal. Our souls need time and attention too, and later on we will talk about forgetting yourself without neglecting yourself. But fixing your eyes on yourself, speaking truth over yourself, affirming yourself, believing in yourself—none of these practices can take you where you want to go. When these messages become the goal, they actually hold you back. You're like a runner sitting on the sidelines, wondering why she hasn't crossed the finish line.

The Great Self-Esteem Flop

If it sounds like I'm being too hard on high self-esteem, researchers have done a lot of work on this subject and they've discovered something surprising.

The term "self-esteem" is relatively new. As recently as a hundred years ago, self-esteem wasn't a thing. Back then, people were more concerned with getting a job that paid the bills than fulfilling their dreams and being their "best self." It wasn't until the Baby Boomer generation that the concept first emerged. That's when people began focusing on goals like "finding themselves" and achieving "self-fulfillment." That was the beginning of the self-esteem movement.

In her book *Generation Me: Why Today's Young Americans Are More Confident, Assertive, Entitled—and More Miserable Than Ever Before*, researcher Jean M. Twenge documents the rise of the self-esteem movement. She notices that between 1940 and 1990, the number of books mentioning self-esteem more than doubled.[5]

Between 1960 and 2008, American books also contained more of the following phrases:

> Just be yourself became 8 times more frequent, learned about myself 4.6 times, believe in yourself 6.5 times, express yourself 2 times, respect yourself 2.7 times, be honest with yourself 3 times, love yourself 5.7 times, I love me 6.7 times, and stand up for yourself 6 times.[6]

As Twenge explains, self-esteem has become a central part of our culture. It shapes the way we parent, it shapes our schools, and it even shapes the church. It is so woven into our thinking that we don't even notice it. Commercials are aimed at creating a "better you" and "making your dreams come true." Books have seen a steady increase in words like *I*, *me*, and *mine*, and in 2013 the *Oxford English Dictionary* declared "selfie" the Word of the Year.[7] The result is a generation of young people who "simply take it for granted that we should all feel good about ourselves, we are all special, and we all deserve to follow our dreams."[8]

Twenge's research is especially interesting because of what it reveals. What started out as a focus on *self-esteem* eventually became a focus on *self*. However, what's even more significant than the derailment of the self-esteem movement is this hard truth:

It failed.

In spite of all the efforts to improve self-esteem and raise a generation of children who like themselves, two things happened:

First, the self-esteem of some young people actually dropped. A 2013 study of girls ages sixteen to eighteen found that their self-esteem is suffering more than girls in the past. The percentage of girls who were unhappy with their appearance rose from 26 percent to 29 percent to 33 percent over a two-year period.[9] Low self-esteem is also one of the most common mental health problems facing girls today, alongside depression and eating disorders. In fact, by the age of fifteen, girls are twice as likely to become depressed as boys.[10]

The second failure of the self-esteem movement is a little less surprising. After all that work to boost self-esteem, some people became self-*absorbed*. Instead of raising people with high self-esteem, we raised narcissists.

In her research, Twenge found that between 1968 and the mid-1990s, the self-esteem of college-aged men and women grew, and in 2008 the average college student had higher self-esteem than 63 percent of students in 1988. She notes, "By 2008, the most frequent self-esteem score for college students was 40—the highest possible score and thus 'perfect' self-esteem."[11] Unfortunately, the rise in high self-esteem has not turned out to be a good thing. The *New York Times* published an article called "The Trouble with Self-Esteem" that explained, "People with high self-esteem pose a greater threat to those around them than people with low self-esteem, and feeling bad about yourself is not the cause of our country's biggest, most expensive social problems."[12] In fact, some researchers wonder if low self-esteem is the lesser of two evils.

The self-esteem movement didn't achieve what our society hoped. Its message of healing is not entirely unhelpful, but it's also limited in its helpfulness. It never gets to the root of the problem.

For many of us, the problem is not that we think poorly about ourselves. The problem is that we can't *stop* thinking about ourselves. All this talk about self-esteem and being our truest and best selves has turned the world into one giant mirror pointing back at us.

That's why self-forgetfulness, not high self-esteem, is the answer.

Easier Said than Done

Unfortunately, a lot of us are stuck staring in the mirror. The mirror reflex is subtle, so it's easy to miss. We assume that, because we're not blatantly selfish, we must not be focused on ourselves. But as I said, the mirror reflex is a human reflex. Most of us find ways to insert ourselves, our reputations, our pride, our identities, into any given situation. Just like that lunch with my college mentor, we're staring at ourselves and we don't even realize it.

In his grace, God opened my eyes to see what my people-pleasing had become. I realized how many of my insecurities and fears could be traced back to an unhealthy focus on myself. I was a distracted runner. I couldn't sprint toward the prize because my eyes were fixed inward, so I decided to get a new focus. I was done living for me, my reputation, my glory. I wanted the freedom of self-forgetfulness.

What I soon discovered is that self-forgetfulness is hard, because self-focus is a human default. It's not enough simply to want self-forgetfulness, or to affirm it and call it good. Self-forgetfulness comes through intentionality, and it takes time, but its fruit is freedom.

I want that for you. I want you to get beyond the point of self-help faith. Too many of us are stuck on the sidelines because we have turned something good into something ultimate. Self-care, though important, is not why we exist, and feeling good about ourselves is not the prize.

In the next section we're going to look at seven different areas of our lives—seven "mirrors"—that we often make "about us." Each chapter will look at the consequences of making things about us that are not about us, and each comes from my own struggle with self-focus. In the final section, "How to Be Free of Me," I'm going to share practical steps toward self-forgetfulness. These practices, along with the power of the Holy Spirit, have given me one of the greatest liberations of my life, which is why I am so eager to share them with you. I hope and pray these practices will set you free.

Now, let's get started.

Focus Verse

"Let your eyes look straight ahead; fix your gaze directly before you."—Proverbs 4:25

Focus Prayer

Loving Father, my focus is fickle. It drifts away from you again and again, no matter how hard I try. I want to live for you, and I want to keep my eyes on you, but I cannot do it without you. I ask for your mercy and your grace. I ask for your Holy Spirit to stand in the gaps. Help me to fix my eyes on you, and thank you for your promise to do it. Amen.

Discussion Questions

1. Can you think of a time when affirmation in one area of your life didn't transfer to other areas?
2. In the past, how have you addressed your insecurities? What did you turn to, and what messages did you embrace?
3. If self-focus doesn't always look like selfishness, what does it look like in your life?
4. How has your self-focus led to insecurity?

PART 2

Seven Mirrors

three

When You Make
God about You

The glory of God is a human being fully alive; and to be alive consists of beholding God.[1]

—St. Irenaeus

*Y*ou are loved." "You are gifted." "God has a plan for you." These are good, true, and biblical messages, but sometimes I wonder: what if we have taken these truths and broken them just a little?

This thought occurred to me one evening as I sat in the basement of a church building, surrounded by a circle of women. I was right in the middle of my confidence crisis, so I had joined a church small group, anxious for affirmation. I needed truth, and I hoped this group would provide it. Our group leader had chosen a book about embracing yourself and acknowledging your God-given beauty. Its message was rooted in biblical truths: God created us in his image, he loves us, and his purpose for us is perfect. The author of the book encouraged us to turn our insecurities over to God, knowing that God made us with intimate intention and calls us good. Only then would we be able to love ourselves and experience freedom.

I listened as the women began discussing the first chapter. They loved it. It resonated with all of them. It was a truth each of them needed to hear, and I was glad for the encouragement they found. One of my favorite things in life is to watch God's truth do what it does best: give hope, freedom, and strength.

And yet.

The message had not resonated with me. It wasn't that I disagreed with the message or that I struggled to believe it. I knew God loved me, and I knew God created me with a purpose. I also knew there were many, *many* people who needed that message. Countless men and women struggle to recognize the image of God in themselves.

Even so, the message of the book felt incomplete, just short of touching the ache inside me. I sat there thinking, "Yes. Yes! And . . . ?"

To be honest, I have felt that way for a long time. For years I've felt a tension about how Christians discuss self-esteem. On the one hand, we need to know what the Bible says about us. Every day we are confronted with lies about who we are and what we're worth. The world tells us that our value comes from our looks, our possessions, our family, or our success, and God's Word challenges these lies with life-giving truth. The gospel takes the heavy burdens of the world and replaces them with freedom in Christ. In every way, the message of God speaks into our lives, shapes our identities, and transforms the way we see ourselves. That is a big part of what it means to be a child of God.

Still, I can't help but wonder if we have taken a good truth and broken it ever so slightly. What if we have taken a truth that sets us free and twisted it or distorted it just enough so that it's no longer freeing?

In her book *Women of the Word: How to Study the Bible with Both Our Hearts and Our Minds*, author Jen Wilkin notices this twisting. She describes how it played out in her own life, confessing that she used to approach the Bible by asking, "Who am I?" and "How can God help me?"—questions the Bible does indeed answer. But, she admits, the real motive behind her question was "a subtle misunderstanding about the very nature of the Bible: I believed that the Bible was a book about me."[2]

Wilkin goes on to explain that Moses made a similar mistake. When God instructed him to go and speak to Pharaoh, Moses was filled with self-doubt. He worried, "*Who am I* that I should go to Pharaoh?" By posing the questions in that order, Moses placed himself at the center of the story. God responded by gently correcting Moses and placing himself back at the center: "*I* will be with you," a statement Wilkin summarizes this way:

> [God] answers Moses's self-focused question of "Who am I?" with the only answer that matters: "I am."[3]

Wilkin's words were another lightbulb moment for me. All those messages I had been hearing—about how special I was and how God had a perfect plan for me—I was taking them and breaking them a little. I was turning the Bible into a book about *me*. I was turning God into a God about *me*. My eyes were focused on *me*. I had made God into a mirror, and although the image was a positive one—and a truthful one—I was still living for myself. Instead of running toward the prize of Christ, I was bumping into the wall of my own reflection.

I was treating God and the Bible as if they were all about me, which made my faith small and powerless. I think a lot of us make the same mistake, but we are by no means the first. After combing through Scripture and reflecting on my life, I discovered four different forms of this false, me-centered god: the self-help god, the self-serving god, the self-exalting god, and the self-image god. Naming these gods is the first step in refocusing on the one true God.

The Self-Help God

The self-help god exists to make you feel better about yourself. If you're feeling lonely, unattractive, overlooked, or insecure, this god can make you feel special. This approach to God is a Christian version of self-help messages, which Jean Twenge (the psychologist I mentioned in the last chapter) noticed in her own research. Her book was not about Christianity per se, but even she observed how the church has adopted the language.

What is really interesting about the Christian self-help approach is that it's markedly different from God's. Returning to Wilkin's example of Moses's self-doubt, Moses felt inhibited by his weaknesses. He didn't feel capable of speaking to Pharaoh or of leading the Israelites out of Egypt, because he only saw his disqualifications. And how did God respond to Moses's doubt? Not with a self-help pep talk. He didn't affirm Moses's leadership or his talents or gifts. He didn't hug him and cheer for him and speak encouraging words over him. God didn't do any of those things, but instead he changed the subject. God affirmed his own strength, his own leadership, his own self, because the outcome never hinged upon Moses. This story was not about Moses's strengths, and Moses was never meant to be the hero. Only God could deliver the Israelites out of Egypt, so he directed Moses's focus back to him.

God responded similarly when he appointed Jeremiah, a prophet who was concerned about his youth. "I do not know how to speak; I am too young," he worried (Jer. 1:6), but God didn't coddle or dote on him. Rather than assure Jeremiah he was talented for his age, that he had great leadership skills and a terrific personality, God simply affirmed his own self: "Do not be afraid of them, for *I am* with you and will rescue you" (1:8). Once again, God directed his servant off of his own limitations and onto the limitless God.

God cares about our insecurities, and his Word does address them, but the difference between a self-help god and the true, living God is focus. The one true God responds to our insecurities with reassurances about himself. In doing so, he releases us from the source of our paralysis, shifting our gaze from the "can'ts" to the One who can.

The Self-Serving God

The self-serving god exists to serve you, to make your life easier and better. This version of God gives you every desire of your heart and makes all your dreams come true. He wants you to be comfortable and happy, even successful and wealthy. This version of God is all about what God can do for you.

Acts 8 tells us of a man who viewed God this same way. His name was Simon and he was a sorcerer. At first Simon seemed to understand who God was, because he heard the message of Jesus and then he was baptized. Eventually, Simon's true motives showed through when he offered to pay the apostles for their powers: "Give me also this ability so that everyone on whom I lay my hands may receive the Holy Spirit" (v. 19). To this offer, Peter responded harshly:

> *May your money perish with you, because you thought you could buy the gift of God with money! You have no part or share in this ministry, because your heart is not right before God. Repent of this wickedness and pray to the Lord in the hope that he may forgive you for having such a thought in your heart. For I see that you are full of bitterness and captive to sin. (vv. 20–23)*

Peter saw through Simon's motives. Simon didn't want God but God's power. Simon was following Jesus not out of love, but because of what Jesus could do for him.

What is especially interesting about Peter's words is his accusation of "bitterness." There is nothing in the passage that hints at this, so you have to wonder why Peter said it. My hunch is that Peter spotted the early seeds of bitterness, because bitterness is the fruit of believing God owes you. We witness this bitterness in the prodigal son's brother, who begrudged his father's mercy (Luke 15:11–32). If you believe faith is payment for living a moral life, bitterness will creep in whenever life doesn't work out. That doesn't mean we can't feel anger about tragedy—the Psalms give us plenty of freedom for that!—but bitterness is an anger we welcome to stay. Bitterness is the anger we nurture and cultivate, until it grows into something toxic and consuming. Rather than making a way for healing, bitterness produces even more woundedness.

Sometimes it's hard to know if you've made God into this self-serving kind of god, but bitterness, hardness, and entitlement are its fruits. How you respond to God when your plans don't work out, or how you respond to Scripture when it challenges your lifestyle—these responses are a litmus test of the kind of god you follow.

The Self-Exalting God

This version of God is about your reputation and your glory. The self-exalting god exists to make you look good in public. You follow this god so that everyone will like you and think you're a good person. The self-exalting god also exists to make you well-known. If you're a pastor, a speaker, a musician, or a writer, it's tempting to treat Jesus as a key to success, "for his glory."

This false god has been one of my biggest struggles, and it's also the one that stole my joy. In the beginning, I didn't pursue ministry in order to be famous, but glory is a seducer, and praise is addictive. The more affirmation I received for my work, the more I needed to have it. Over time, the desire became a lifestyle.

In Mark 10, James and John ask Jesus if one of them can "sit at your right and the other at your left in your glory" (v. 37), and the timing of their question reveals their own idolatry. Just prior to asking this question, Jesus had predicted his own death. In the clearest terms possible, he warned that his call was to sacrifice and not to status. But the disciples missed the message. They were too caught up in jockeying for position and fighting for glory.

It would be easy to sit in judgment over the disciples' vainglory, if this wasn't a lifelong struggle of mine. My desire for glory is one I can't seem to shake, and for years I have begged God to remove it. The one truth that has comforted me (and which is true of all these false gods) is that the self-exalting god isn't rotten to the core. It's merely a distortion of something good. In his book *The Weight of Glory*, C. S. Lewis explains that seeking glory is not in itself wrong, depending on who we seek it from. The desire for praise can be pure, like a child beckoning her father, "Daddy, look! Look what I did!"[4] A child's longing for praise is God-given, and it's also a foretaste of heaven. As Lewis describes it, there will come a day "when the redeemed learn at last that we have pleased him whom we were created to please."[5] Our desire for glory is a desire given to us; God created us to seek praise from him.

I love Lewis's perspective because of what it means about God: unlike us, he *shares* his glory. Human glory is typically selfish and competitive, but God's glory is a generous glory. Romans 8:17 explains, "We share in his sufferings in order that we may also share in his glory," which means we get to enjoy God's glory *with* him. We can and should seek God's praise, but approval is only sweet if it directs our attention back to him.

The Self-Image God

In her book *Bird by Bird*, Anne Lamott shares these wise words, which were imparted to her by a friend: "You can safely assume you've created God in your own image when it turns out that God hates all the same people you do."[6] This is the self-image god, or "God in the image of self."

This version of God is, in some ways, a combination of all the others. It serves you, exalts you, and affirms who you are, because this version of God looks just like you. This god cares about the rules you care about. This god supports the causes you support. This god judges the people you judge. And this god has a *lot* of grace in the areas where you struggle. This version of God is also the hardest to see, because the differences between God's convictions and ours are tough to admit or even recognize.

There is no better example of a self-image god than the one constructed by the Pharisees. The Pharisees knew the Law backward and forward. They were the experts, and they were strict. Because God commanded us to rest on the Sabbath, they had a list of thirty-nine prohibited activities. Lighting a fire, clapping your hands, slapping your thighs, even visiting the sick—all were banned on the Sabbath.[7] This, they believed, was what God wanted.

Somewhere along the way the Pharisees had missed the point. Rather than practicing these rules as a way to honor God, they treated the rules as God. Their interpretation of Scripture became *the* interpretation, which meant anyone who rebelled against them was rebelling against God himself. That is exactly how these religious leaders, who were supposed to know God best, failed to recognize him in their midst: he didn't look like *them*. In Luke 13, Jesus healed a crippled woman on the Sabbath, and the religious leaders were scandalized. "That's work!" they accused. "We're supposed to rest today!" Their response exposed the disconnect between their rules and God's heart, and in verses 15–16, Jesus rebuked them: "You take care of your ox on the Sabbath, but you judge me for healing a human being?" (paraphrase).

This double standard seems obvious today. *Of course* you should help someone on the Sabbath. And yet many of us do the very same thing whenever we judge other Christians against a "list"— the way they parent, the movies they see, the way they dress, the politicians they vote for, or anything that is different from us. We must be wary of making God into our own image.

When we make God into our own image, we end up opposing God instead. That's the lesson we take from the Pharisees, and it's a sobering truth for sure. It makes me want to see God—all of him—but especially the parts of myself that are most unlike him. Only then can I identify the strongholds and broken places that stand between me and Christ. Viewing God in the image of myself might feel comfortable and affirming, and it might give me a perch to look down on others, but it will not give me life.

When we make God about us, we miss something essential about him *and* ourselves. The "special sauce" of the gospel is not that it makes us feel good, but that it calls us into something bigger than ourselves. That larger vision is the thing our souls crave, but a domesticated god cannot provide it. In order to hold onto that bigger story, we have to live for much more than our own story. That means focusing on more than what God can do for us, and focusing simply on God.

The One True God

As long as I have been a Christian, one story in the Bible has inspired me more than any other. No matter how many times I read it I can hardly believe it, and I'm talking about the book of Philippians. What makes Philippians powerful is its backstory, since Paul wrote this letter from prison. His future was uncertain, and his rivals—Christians!—were capitalizing on his imprisonment. But this context is what makes Paul's message so amazing. Rather than despair or grow bitter, Paul chose to rejoice, using the word "joy" more times here than in any of his other letters. This prison epistle is a master class in contentment.

Paul's joy is remarkable, but it also begs the question: how did he do it? How did he hold onto his joy? The answer lies in Philippians 1:15–18:

> It is true that some preach Christ out of envy and rivalry, but others out of goodwill. The latter do so out of love, knowing that I am put here for the defense of the gospel. The former preach Christ out of selfish ambition, not sincerely, supposing that they can stir up trouble for me while I am in chains. But what does it matter? The important thing is that in every way, whether from false motives or true, Christ is preached. And because of this I rejoice.

Paul's joy was rock solid because it stood on solid rock. His joy didn't rest on his success or his reputation or the opinions of others. He wasn't bothered by criticism—even from other Christians—because he didn't care about his glory, but God's.

I don't know about you, but I dream of having such a focus, which is why I'm going to use Paul as a touchstone in this book. The freedom Paul had is what we were created for, and it can't be bound by literal chains or self-imposed ones. It's a freedom so all-encompassing, so unlike anything else in this world, that it almost seems like a miracle.

Paul got it. He understood the gospel in a way that set him free, even from behind his prison walls. He lived as a man with nothing to lose, and that's a lightness only Jesus can give. In the final chapters of this book, we will look at practical steps toward the freedom that Paul possessed, but for now, let me give you a taste, because it can all be summed up with these words:

> *"Love the Lord your God with all your heart and with all your soul and with all your strength and with all your mind"; and, "Love your neighbor as yourself."* (Luke 10:27)

Paul's life and spiritual freedom were an embodiment of these words. This was his secret, and this is our goal. It's what we were created for, it's where freedom lives, and we will return to these words again and again, because everything in our lives that we make about us was all intended for this.

Focus Verse

"And we all, who with unveiled faces contemplate the Lord's glory, are being transformed into his image with ever-increasing glory."—2 Corinthians 3:18

Focus Prayer

Loving Father, teach me to see you. Teach me to gaze on you and to know you, not simply for my own gain, but for the sake of you alone. Thank you for creating a world in which we are changed, healed, and redeemed as we seek you, but protect me from making myself the starting point. Help me to focus on you and to live for you, for your glory and my freedom. Amen.

Discussion Questions

1. Of the four false gods listed (self-help god, self-serving god, self-exalting god, and self-image god), which resonated with you most?

2. How have these false gods affected you negatively?

3. What are some of the ways we can sort out the "one true God" from the false gods that we make about us?

4. How did you feel about Paul's unflappable joy? Does it feel attainable or unrealistic?

four

When You Make Family about You

The strength and happiness of families is an important thing.
But it is a byproduct of service to a kingdom.[1]

—Rodney Clapp

*I*ke and I sat next to each other on a burgundy couch. A space heater buzzed in the corner and snow was falling outside. It was a cold Chicago winter day, so I tucked my legs underneath me and held my coffee close. It was cozy and comfortable in that tiny room, which is a funny thing to say about your marriage counselor's office.

Before we even got married, Ike and I decided to make counseling a priority. As a child of divorce, Ike knew healthy marriages take work. Marriage for life doesn't happen on its own, so we decided to address our issues head-on, before they became *issues.* Not long after our wedding, we began a monthly routine of visiting our counselor, and she has become a wonderful part of our lives.

On that particular day, I wanted to discuss something that happened over the weekend. We had attended a dinner party with some friends, and at some point during the night I thought Ike was being too loud. In hindsight, it was nothing at all, but at the time I felt embarrassed, so I made a snide remark. I wanted to distance myself from his actions. Of course, that only made things worse. My comment embarrassed him, so he fired right back, and we argued the entire ride home.

As we rehashed the incident, our counselor identified the core of my embarrassment. She used a term I had never heard—and one I will never forget—because it's about so much more than marriage. She called it **image management**, and it's exactly how it sounds: when you "manage" how people see you. It takes an endless number of forms, like the need to appear attractive, happy, successful, organized, or smart, and just like the mirror reflex, it treats everything in your life as a reflection on you.

You might be able to guess how complicated this becomes when image management shapes your relationships. For most of us, it starts in our teen years when we are hypervigilant about our reputation. I will never forget my dad predicting that one day I would be too cool for him. "Once you're in high school, you'll think you're smarter than me, and you won't want to be seen with me in public."

"No way!" I protested. I was eight years old and thought my parents hung the moon. "I would never do that!" I promised.

Seven years later, I proved my dad right by being mortified at my parents' sense of humor. If they made a lame joke in front of my friends, I made sure to distance myself from them. I needed my friends to know that *I knew* it was lame, so I rolled my eyes and heaved out long, agonized sighs.

Most of us outgrow this phase of our teens, but we don't outgrow the tendency to manage our image. Instead it becomes heightened and more destructive, especially in marriage and parenting. When our spouse or our kids become extensions of us, they are forced to bear a burden that was never theirs to carry. It's a toxic dynamic for relationships, and that's exactly what was happening between me and Ike. I wasn't responding out of love for him, but out of love for myself. I was managing my image, which meant I had to manage him.

Image management is one of the ways we treat family like a mirror. Rather than seeing *them*—who they are, what they need, and how to love them—we see ourselves, our aspirations, and our fears. It's not hard to guess why this habit is dangerous, but in this chapter we're going to take a look. We'll examine three family relationships—with our spouse, our kids, and our parents—and what happens when we make them about us.

Mirror Marriage

When I was in my midtwenties, I worked as a college minister at a local school. One afternoon, a freshman dropped by my office wanting to talk about life. She was a natural leader with loads of charisma, but she had never had a boyfriend and was worried. She wondered if there was something wrong with her, and was concerned that she might never get married.

I listened sympathetically because I knew how she felt. At the time, I was twenty-eight and newly engaged. I lived in the South, where people marry young, so I was bringing up the tail end of my friends. I had watched each one of them marry before me, and for years I feared my time would never come.

For me, the antidote to fear was adventure. I traveled, went on mission trips, earned a master's degree, and lived to the fullest. My motto during that season was "No regrets." I wanted to look back and feel proud of what I did. Rather than waste my single-ness waiting around for a husband, I wanted to take advantage of being unattached. And I did. I didn't have any regrets, and I am still grateful for that season of my life. I wouldn't have changed a thing.

I shared my story with her and encouraged her to dream. "Use this season while you have it! Instead of worrying about the future, invest in the life you have now!" I thought it was a really great speech. Soon we wrapped up our conversation and she walked to the door, before turning on her heel and pronouncing, "I just hope I don't have to wait to get married until I'm twenty-eight. That would be AWFUL."

Well.

My advice had not inspired her, but I share this story because of what it symbolizes. For many Christians, marital status is a measure of worth. Single Christians hear this message the loudest because of the attention churches often give to families, as if to say families have a higher priority. As a result of this messaging, image management begins long before the wedding. As singles, many of us wrestle with the connection between self-image and relation-ship status. Some singles bounce from relationship to relationship, while others become defiantly independent. But most, at some time or another, ask questions like, *Why am I single? What does my singleness say about me? Is there something wrong with me?* There is a temptation to believe singleness says something *about you*, which is why most single people consider these questions.

The heartache of singleness is normal, because the desire to marry is good. Regardless of whether you marry, the desire for marriage is God-given. This good desire only goes awry when we link relationship status to self-image. If our self-image is tied to being with someone, then we are nurturing image management from the start. Marriage will not somehow eradicate the habit, but will only expand it to include your spouse. How he behaves in social settings, how she speaks to you in front of others, her job, his hobbies, her interests, his jokes, it all gets run through the filter of image management. This tendency is easy to spot in newly married or dating couples. A husband makes a bad pun, and his wife's body language says it all: "I do not endorse." This is classic image management.

Image management might seem relatively harmless, but there are a few reasons why it's unhealthy. First, it places unfair pressure on your relationship by saddling your spouse with your own insecurities. Second, it is dishonoring to your spouse. Image management rarely expresses itself graciously. It is more likely to come out in the form of condescension, sarcasm, or plain old meanness. Third, it diminishes your spouse. Rather than appreciating your spouse for who they are, you are constantly judging them. You can't enjoy them for who they are, and you might even wind up belittling them.

As for singles, I asked some of my single friends how they see image management playing out in their lives, and how it negatively affects their relationships. One admitted to dating men she wasn't especially interested in, or flirting with men she had no intention of dating, simply to receive positive feedback. Another described initially rejecting a wonderful guy because he didn't measure up to her image. Still another explained the urge to offset the absence of a family by posting photos of herself looking independent and full of life. All of them, at some time or another, battled an appearance of incompleteness, which sometimes led them to make bad decisions and hurt the people around them.

That's why image management is bad for marriages, dating relationships, and singleness. When we make marriage and relationship status about us, we focus on ourselves instead of others, which prevents us from loving people well. Sometimes we even end up using them.

One of the first steps to avoiding image management is simply to name it. Knowing about this habit is powerful, because you will begin to recognize it when you're doing it. Later in this chapter, we will look at God's intention for family, which offers us a beautiful alternative to our self-focused approaches. But first, let's look at how image management seeps into parenting.

Mirror Parenting

My oldest son was born eleven days late, and I'm convinced he needed every minute of it. He was perfectly healthy and ready for the world, but he only weighed five pounds and twelve ounces. Since that day he has remained on the small side, and I didn't think much of it until the day I brought him in for a physical. He was two years old, and his height and weight percentiles had dropped a few points. The doctor turned to me with a furrowed brow and asked, "Are you feeding him enough?"

"I think so?" I replied, my confidence wobbling. "He eats all the time . . . I give him food whenever he's hungry . . . He seems to be getting enough?" The more I defended myself, the more uncertain I felt. All this time I thought I was doing a good job! But now the doctor had me questioning myself. Was I the reason for his size?

To some extent, the answer is yes, because I am a petite person and my husband isn't large. Neither of us carries the genes of a seven-foot linebacker. And yet, the doctor's tone made me wonder. Maybe his size was my *fault*. Maybe I had been raising him wrong. Maybe his size said something about me.

My son's size is a fairly low-stakes example, but I think most parents have been there. Your child throws a tantrum in the canned goods aisle, and you instantly feel judged by the world. Your child bites another child, picks on a kid at school, disobeys a teacher, or doesn't start reading as soon as her peers, and each one feels like a referendum on your parenting.

It's a natural reaction, but it's one we must fight. In the same way that image management puts an unfair burden on our marriages, it similarly affects our kids. When image management steers our parenting, our kids become responsible for their reputation *and* our reputation, their insecurities *and* our insecurities, their fears *and* our fears. And just like marriage, this makes for a toxic parent-child relationship. Maybe you have even been on the child's end of this dynamic, so you know exactly how it feels. Your mom criticized you or your dad pressured you, and as much as it hurt, you also wondered if some of those criticisms were more about them than you.

If that has been your own experience, let me speak this truth over you: *that is NOT about you.* And more importantly, that is not how God parents. Our God rejoices over us with singing (see Zeph. 3:17) and lays himself down to make us whole, not the other way around. When your parent puts his or her insecurities on your back, I would encourage you to name it for what it is, forgive them, and then ask God for the grace to stop the cycle with your own kids.

Now, before we take a closer look at image management in parenting, I want to acknowledge how mirror parenting affects people without children. One of the subtle consequences of making our kids about us is that it shapes how we talk about parenthood. More precisely, it causes us to elevate parenting to incredible heights. Church leaders describe parenting as the greatest of all callings, which creates a system of rank. For those individuals who don't have children, or are unable to, their role in the church seems less valuable.

For some of my Christian friends, this message has been painful. We need to do better, not only because this message is hurtful, but because it's also untrue. Whether we have children or simply hope to, children are not the fulfillment of our identities, and they should never be asked to bear that weight. The Christian identity can stand on no person—spouse or child—but on Jesus Christ alone. That means that in the same breath, we can both affirm the desire to have children and denounce the ways we use children as a measure of a worthy life. For the sake of our kids and the sake of all the non-parents who feel marginalized by the church, let's be diligent about both.

For those of us who do have kids, or hope to one day, what happens when we make our kids about us? There are a number of different consequences, but I want to focus on three of the most immediate ones. If you recognize these symptoms in your parenting and in your heart, then it's a good sign you have made parenting about you.

The first is **pressure**. When we make our kids about us, we feel pressure to be great parents, and as a result, we put pressure on our kids to succeed. You see this in parents who push their kids to be first, best, or fastest. And it starts so young! My oldest son is only four, and I already wonder if I need to enroll him in more extracurricular activities or a more rigorous preschool—you know, for college. Whenever I find out my friends' children are writing or reading or doing math, I nearly break out in hives. Then I talk myself down with truths like, "He will figure out how to read eventually," and "Whatever his strengths might be, I need to be patient in discerning them," and also "Get a grip!"

The second consequence of making our kids about us is **guilt**. For many of us, guilt sets in before our children are even born. As soon as the pregnancy test comes back positive, we discover a list of things we "should" be doing to care for our future offspring: no caffeine, no soft cheeses, no deli meats, no sushi, no wine. And then there are all the *choices*, each one presenting itself like a pass-fail test: disposable diapers or cloth diapers? Store-bought baby food or homemade baby food? Attachment parenting or sleep training? The list goes on and on, and we make our choices, and for just a moment we feel good about them. Until the day we are confronted with a parent who makes different choices, who goes above and beyond, who not only makes the baby food but breastfeeds for two years instead of one. The parent who doesn't seem to need any time away from her kids and never *ever* allows her kids screen time. In that moment, instead of thinking, "Good for her!" we are more likely to think one of two things: (1) *Why is she making it so hard for the rest of us?* or (2) *I need to do better.* Whenever we glimpse a parent who has chosen a different style than ours, it instantly feels like a measuring stick.

I struggle with this a lot. When I pacify my children with Netflix on my phone, I feel the eyes of other parents silently judging me. Or rather, I *assume* they are. In reality no one thinks about me that much, because most people are just doing the best they can. In fact, most people aren't thinking about you or me at all, because they are focused on their own lives and their own families. It's an important reminder on those days when every other parent seems better prepared than you. We tend to focus on the things other parents are doing well, like teaching their kids sign language, or taking them to music class, or doing crafts with their recycled egg cartons. But when we do this—when we focus on other parents' successes and our failures—it leaves us feeling like second-string parents. And when we treat our kids like a reflection of ourselves, they get wrapped up into our constant need to be "enough."

If guilt is your particular struggle, I want you to know one of the many reasons we refer to Jesus's life, death, and resurrection as "good news." Jesus died on a cross in the place of all humanity—you, me, everyone—and his death was the great reckoning for our guilt. For all who believe in him, it is finished. Our sin and brokenness has been accounted for and reconciled. Jesus took our guilt upon himself to set us free from it, and walking in that truth means we don't have to feel guilty all the time. Some of our guilt is self-inflicted—such as guilt over our kids' mismatched clothes, or guilt over a messy house—but even when our guilt is based on real sin, it is all covered in Christ. Living in a state of constant guilt is living as if Jesus never died.

Here is the even better news: Jesus didn't just take our guilt. His grace is bigger than that. Even when we make honest mistakes or run up against our own human limitations, God's grace fills in the cracks. He covers our sins and our innocent shortcomings, which means "Christian parenting" is not perfect parenting, but parenting under the grace of Christ. Our call is not to be flawless parents, but to point to the Parent who never disappoints.

The last consequence of self-focused parenting is, surprisingly, **self-neglect**. There is a brand of parenting, especially prevalent among moms, that equates parenting with martyrdom. It's the idea that the best moms would do anything—*anything*—for their children, which sounds like a legacy worth having. I'm going to address this more in a later chapter, but for now I will say this: running yourself into the ground is no measure of your effectiveness as a parent. More often, it points to overcommitment, disorganization, and even disobedience. I know that last one sounds harsh, but remember, God *commands* us to rest (Exod. 20:8). The Sabbath isn't just a divine expectation, but a divine order for our own well-being. Sometimes self-neglect exposes a neglect of this command.

If self-neglect is your issue, if the need to be an "exceptional" parent has left you exhausted and dry, I want you to know that self-neglect is not the same as godly sacrifice. Sometimes God does call us to sacrifice for our kids, and that kind of sacrifice does echo the perfect sacrifice of our heavenly Father. However, there is a kind of sacrifice that is self-serving. This kind of sacrifice is about you more than it is about your kids. Perhaps it is the need to be seen a certain way, or the desire to prove you can do it all, but it slowly eats away at your peace. Godly sacrifice will not do that, so we need godly community and the Holy Spirit to help us discern between the two. Because not all sacrifice is an act of love. Parenting for the glory of God is exhausting at times, but when it's fundamentally about Christ instead of us, the stakes are both higher and lower, weightier and lighter. There is marvelous freedom in having nothing to prove.

Mirror Mom and Dad

We have a story in my family that perfectly represents my mom's approach to parenting. It dates back to my early twenties when I had just graduated from college. I moved back home, began attending a new church, and then, for reasons unknown, I joined the church's softball league. It must have been a desperate attempt to make friends, because I am not athletic and had never played softball in my life.

To make matters worse, this was no ordinary softball team. Several of the players had played baseball in college. Another had played in the *major leagues*. And then there was me, the girl who shut her eyes when she tried to catch the ball. My contribution to the team was literally in the negatives.

For my first game of the season, my parents decided to come support me. They sat in the stands and cheered, while I stood in the outfield filling dead space. Eventually it was my turn to bat, so I walked up to the plate, adjusted my grip, and raised my bat into the air. Suddenly, I heard the high-pitched voice of a woman calling from the stands:

"Go, Sharon! You're the best one on the team!"

In case it isn't obvious, that woman was my mom. In case it isn't also obvious, she was absolutely wrong. I was not the best one on the team. I wasn't even the *seventh* best one on the team. I was the last best one on the team. My mom's assessment of my abilities was empirically false.

But that's how my mom is. I think she sees that as her role, to believe in me. Both my parents have always been that way, sometimes unreasonably so, and it has shaped the way I see myself.

Unlike marriage and parenting, your own parents "reflect you" in a different way. For the first eighteen years of your life, your parents know you better than just about anyone else, so they naturally influence the way you see yourself. How they love you, nurture you, encourage you—or fail to—shapes your self-image profoundly.

If you're like me, and your parents affirmed your identity and accepted you unconditionally, it probably instilled confidence in you. If your parents tore you down, nitpicked, exploded on you, were never satisfied, or were simply absent, it probably shaped your self-image differently. Words like *advanced*, *smart*, *pretty*, *talented*, and *athletic*, or *dumb*, *stupid*, *chubby*, and *slow*, quickly become the foundation of your identity. If your parents know you better than anyone else and that is what they see in you, then it *must* be true.

For most of us, that's our story, but here's what I want you to know: no matter what kind of parents you had, good or bad, you can't treat them like a mirror. That doesn't mean you shouldn't value their feedback, receive their affirmation, honor them, and be open to their criticism, but you should hold it all loosely.

The thing is, it doesn't matter if your parents reflect a positive image or a negative one; the mirror of your parents is usually distorted. Perhaps they're imposing their insecurities on you, or perhaps they're ridiculously biased about your gifts (or softball skills), but either way, the reflection will always be skewed—sometimes a little, and sometimes a lot. I suspect that is one of the many reasons God refers to himself as Father. He knows how tempting it is to rely on our parents for self-understanding. By identifying himself as a parent, he lays claim to that role. He alone is capable of teaching us who we are, not by offering us a mirror but by offering us a vision. The more we gaze on him and pursue him, the more we become ourselves.

God's Vision for Family

Why did God create family? If we want to avoid making marriage and parenting about us, it's important to answer this question. What is family *meant* to be about?

As it turns out, there are a lot of reasons God created the family. In Genesis 2:18, God declares it is "not good" for man to be alone. Additionally, parenting teaches us about our heavenly Father, how to relate to him as his children, and how to relate to one another.[2] Family benefits and sharpens us in an endless number of ways, but it has a larger purpose as well.

In his book *Families at the Crossroads*, author Rodney Clapp has this to say about the purpose of family: "To be healthy, the family needs a mission or purpose beyond itself." That purpose, he explains, is in service to the kingdom of God. This purpose is so important, so essential, that "the family hurts itself when it makes the family the goal and object of Christian mission."[3] In his book *You and Me Forever*, Francis Chan echoes a similar vision: "We have made happy families our mission. That is not the mission that Jesus gave us."[4] Instead, the mission God gave us is to love God and love others, and it all comes down to that. The purpose of family is to love God and others. The purpose of marriage is to love God and others. The purpose of parenting is to love God and others. That's the answer to the question.

We learn to love God and others inside our families, where our hearts are refined by the fires of intimacy and daily life together. However, the strange math of it all is that the better we love our families, the better we will love people outside our families. Love begets love. So we start by loving our families well, not to construct our own little heaven on earth, but because there is a bigger mission in view.

To put it another way, the purpose of your family is not to make you look good. The purpose of your family is not to make you comfortable. And the purpose of your parenting is not to raise successful kids who get ahead of all the other kids. The purpose of your family is to love your kids *and* other kids. The purpose of your family is to love your family *and* other families. The purpose of your marriage is to love God and the world better than you could have done it alone. God gives us these gifts not only to enjoy but to help us step into our broader created purpose.

As Christians, that is our challenge and our call. Family was never meant to be a pawn in the game of image management, because it was never meant to be about us. *For* us, yes. About us, no. Once we get that and really grab hold of God's vision for family, we get to enjoy our families more than ever. When our families are about loving God and others instead of maintaining an image, or comparing ourselves with others, or making sure our kids stay ahead, we don't have to strive anymore. It also releases our children from the society-imposed burden of self-focus. When we invite children into a purpose much larger than themselves, the pressure is so much less.

In 1 Corinthians 7:8, Paul addresses unmarried people and widows, saying, "It is good for them to stay unmarried." In verses 32–34 he explains his logic, arguing, "An unmarried man is concerned about the Lord's affairs—how he can please the Lord," whereas a married man is "concerned about the affairs of this world." There are a number of different ways to apply this teaching, but the principle underneath it is for married and single people alike: there is a calling greater than family. Family is good and beautiful and God-ordained, and it can absolutely participate in the call, but it was never meant to be an end in itself. Whatever we do, and wherever life takes us, the mission is always higher. That mission—not our perfect marriages or successful kids—is what makes Christian families so different.

Focus Verse

"But as for me and my household, we will serve the LORD."— Joshua 24:15

Focus Prayer

Loving Father, thank you for being the perfect parent I never had and the perfect parent I never have to be. Thank you for removing that burden from families and for covering us in your redemptive grace. You model your intention for family, and I ask for the wisdom and conviction to live it out. Give me a vision for my family, and teach me the steps to pursue it. Amen.

Discussion Questions

1. In which areas of your life are you most tempted toward "image management"?
2. How has image management created tension or conflict in your relationships?
3. Are your parents a positive reflection or a negative reflection of you? Or both?
4. What would you say is your family's "mission," or what would you like it to be?

five

When You Make Your Appearance about You

The Christian self-image is never an end in itself. It is always a means to the end of living for God and for others.[1]

—Anthony A. Hoekema

*H*ave you ever seen a pregnant woman who was absolutely adorable? No swollen ankles, no achy back, just darling? Like someone had stuck a small basketball right up under her shirt? Throughout my twenties, that's how I saw all pregnant women in the world. All of them. Precious. Glowing. Gorgeous. I remember walking past the maternity aisle in Target and wanting so badly to wear the trendy tops with elastic in the waist. What is cuter than a woman with a pregnant belly? Nothing, that's what. I could not wait to have my own.

Then I got pregnant. Now, let me begin by saying pregnancy is such a gift. It truly is miraculous, and I am so thankful for the pregnancies I've had. In many ways, pregnancy and childbirth are simply magical. But adorable? No. Not for me, anyways. I did not feel cute. I felt like a whale. I watched in horror as the numbers on the scale increased and the skin on my belly stretched. I felt like a monster.

Throughout my first pregnancy, I literally asked my husband every day if he was still attracted to me. And every day, he assured me that he was: "Sharon, I am actually *more* attracted to you now than ever. Your body is doing this beautiful work!" But I was sure he was lying. How could he be attracted to *all of this*?

After my son was born, my confidence continued to flounder, mostly because my body was forever changed. My hips were wider and my stomach softer. The average person probably wouldn't detect the changes, but I could, and that's all that mattered to me. For the first time in my life, my body wasn't doing what I wanted.

In reality, God was exposing an idol of control. Pregnancy unearthed a brokenness that I didn't know was inside me. Prior to pregnancy, I thought my body image was fantastic. I didn't spend much time thinking about my weight or the size of my clothes, because I was thin. My metabolism was high. I could eat whatever I wanted, and I never gained a pound. Once that ended and I lost control of my body, my idolatry came roaring to the surface.

Pregnancy forced me to grapple with my body in a way I hadn't before. For the first time in my life, I was uncomfortable with my body, and I even disliked it. I complained about my body and was more focused on my body than at any other time in my life.

My preoccupation with appearance eventually came to a head with a timely, gentle wake-up call. It happened one morning when I made a run to the store. It was 7:00 a.m. and we were out of milk, so I decided to make a quick trip. No need to put on makeup, fix my hair, or change into clean clothes. It wasn't like I was going to see anyone I knew.

What happened next is exactly what you would expect to happen: I ran into someone I knew. It was a woman from church, and as soon as I noticed her, I looked for the nearest place to hide. But it was too late: we made eye contact, and I shuffled toward her, walk-of-shame style. Then, as I met her gaze, I noticed a strange look dash across her face. It was quick, barely noticeable, but she had *hesitated*. That look in her eyes was a brief failure of recognition. Without my makeup on, she didn't know who I was.

If you have never experienced what this is like—to be unrecognizable without makeup on—let me tell you, it's not terrific. Basically, I wanted to evaporate. Instead, I smiled and said hello, asked her how she was doing, and then I *apologized* for not having any makeup on. APOLOGIZED. To this day, I have no idea why I did that. Why would I apologize to her for having to see my actual face? As if my real face would be offensive to her. Why?

Whenever I think back on that interaction, I suspect the real person I should apologize to is God, since I was so ashamed of the face he made. To this day I am flabbergasted by my response, but it was the reality check I needed. My preoccupation with my appearance had become a false compass, and I had lost my true north.

Since then, I've had a lot of time to think about why I apologized for my appearance. I have come to realize that my response was actually quite normal. Maybe you have never apologized for your face, but you probably try to keep your weaknesses tucked away. You probably feel exposed when your physical imperfections are noticeable to others. We all do it, and humans have been doing it since Adam and Eve hid their bodies in the garden. It's true of sin and it's true of muffin tops: we camouflage the things we don't like about ourselves.

Now here's where this gets tricky. Body image is not about us, but our bodies are a part of us. We can't separate our exteriors from who we are, because God made each of us to be whole people, body and soul. Our bodies are not all of us, but they are a significant part of us. If our physical bodies weren't important, Jesus wouldn't have taken on physical form. But he did. He took on human flesh so that he could redeem *all* of us, both our bodies *and* our souls.

This means that "what's inside of you" is NOT all that matters to God. Your outside matters too, because everything about you matters to God. Your entire self was created with a purpose, which means your appearance is not the enemy. Your body, your face, your hair, your eyes, all of it is "good." At the beginning of time, God declared it to be so. Where we go wrong is overemphasizing that goodness and making it about us. When appearance becomes a sum-total reflection of our worth, that's when things go haywire.

Broken Beauty

A few years ago, I attended a women's event at my church, and it was fancy. Unlike my ill-fated milk run, I was looking pretty good. I had showered. I had curled my hair. I was wearing a dress. I was ready to be *seen*.

As soon as I walked through the door, I ran into a friend of mine. I gave her a hug and started to ask about her week, when she leaned back, scanned my outfit, and sighed, "Wow, you look so cute! You always look so cute."

Her words were intended as a compliment, but they made my stomach turn. Behind them I detected feelings of inferiority, failure, and insecurity. She had a newborn at home and had barely made it out the door, so dressing up was out of the question. Church should have been a refuge, but instead she was confronted with comparison. All around her were cute, accessorized women whose appearances spotlighted her inadequacy. And I was one of them.

Her words stopped me dead in my tracks. They left me wondering what it would look like to love her well in her current season of life. It's a delicate question to answer because on one level, insecurity is an issue of the heart. For each and every one of us, insecurity points to our own broken vision. It causes us to see perfection that simply isn't there, which means no one can "make" us feel insecure. Much of that struggle is between us and God.

And yet, my friend's struggle isn't unique. Her form of insecurity is pandemic. *Most* women struggle with body image and comparison, because it's a part of the air we breathe. Nearly everywhere we turn, we encounter messages about beauty and commercials designed to make us feel dissatisfied with ourselves.

Not surprisingly, these messages are taking a toll. In 2011, *Glamour* magazine conducted a survey of 300 women in which 97 percent of the participants admitted to feeling body dissatisfaction at some point during the day. On average, women also reported having thirteen negative thoughts about their body each day.[2] Another survey of 4,023 women, conducted by *SELF* magazine, found that 80 percent of the women were dissatisfied with their bodies, while only 14 percent reported "liking" the way their bodies looked.[3]

As a result of these damaging influences, roughly 75 percent of women engage in "some unhealthy thoughts, feelings or behaviors related to food or their bodies."[4] In 2013, women also had more than 10.3 million surgical and nonsurgical cosmetic procedures, signifying a 471 percent increase since 1997.[5]

With cultural influences like this, it's no wonder most women are dissatisfied—and preoccupied—with their bodies. The trouble is, when we succumb to the pressure of culture, we end up participating in it. Rather than lower the bar for other women, we raise it even higher.

That's why my friend's insecurity was not simply "her problem." There is a very real sense in which women are doing this *to* one another. When we make our bodies *about us*, we contribute to the culture of competition. When we make our appearances *about us*, our desire to look cute is what dictates our actions, instead of our desire to love.

The truth is, when we make our bodies about us, it's bad for us and the women around us. It helps no one. That's why we need to reclaim God's vision for appearance.

Jesus and Self-Image

Jesus cared about his appearance. I know that sounds funny, but it's true, though not in a worldly sense. In Philippians 2, Paul says this about Christ:

> *Have this mind among yourselves, which is yours in Christ Jesus, who, though he was in the form of God, did not count equality with God a thing to be grasped, but emptied himself, by taking the form of a servant, being born in the likeness of men. And being found in human form, he humbled himself by becoming obedient to the point of death, even death on a cross.* (vv. 5–8 ESV)

When Jesus came down to earth, he had a choice to make. He could descend in all his glory, he could live the life of a king, and he could be handsome, strong, and dashing.

But he didn't. Why?

There are a lot of reasons Jesus took on human form, but one of them is this: he was breaking down barriers between himself and us. Jesus relinquished his splendor so that he could enter into people's lives. He wanted people to feel welcome in his presence, so he treated his appearance as a bridge. He rejected the prevailing expectations of glory and power, and took an appearance that best positioned him to love and connect with others.

In 1 Corinthians 9, Paul adopted a similar strategy. He writes,

> *Though I am free and belong to no one, I have made myself a slave to everyone, to win as many as possible. To the Jews I became like*

a Jew, to win the Jews. To those under the law I became like one under the law (though I myself am not under the law), so as to win those under the law. To those not having the law I became like one not having the law (though I am not free from God's law but am under Christ's law), so as to win those not having the law. To the weak I became weak, to win the weak. I have become all things to all people so that by all possible means I might save some. (vv. 19–22)

What Jesus and Paul both understood is that everything about us was created for love. Our bodies and our souls were given to us for love—the love of God and the love of others. The challenge, then, is not to forget our appearances or to downplay them, but to remember what they are for. And what they are *not* for. Too often, appearance becomes a relational barrier, when God intended it as a bridge.

Compassion over Comparison

What does it look like, practically, to view our appearance as a bridge? How can we recruit our whole selves into the mission of love? In their book, *Wild and Free*, Jess Connelly and Hayley Morgan have one answer. It's tucked away in a challenge to their readers, but when I read it, it leapt off the page. They encourage women to "choose compassion over comparison,"[6] and that is a big chunk of the work.

The word *compassion* literally means "to suffer with," and recalling Philippians 2, this choice is the legacy of Christ. He denied himself glory and lowered himself, instead of merely affirming us from afar. He didn't speak love and truth while remaining distant and pristine on his throne. He came down, put on a humble appearance, and got on our level.

In our culture of image, Christ's humility is our example. If we want to resist a culture that makes women feel small because of how they look, if we really want to challenge that message and love women well, then it's not enough to affirm our sisters without changing the way we live. No matter what we say, no matter how passionate or heartfelt, we can't reverse the cultural tide while also playing into it. Jesus knew this. He couldn't overturn worldly power by playing into worldly power. So he came in the form of a fragile baby, born in a manger, the son of a carpenter. This "King of the Jews" looked nothing like a king, and that's where the revolution began.

Likewise, the way to love women in a culture of impossible standards is to reject those impossible standards by humbling ourselves. We have to choose compassion over comparison, and compassion over competition. Does that mean we should auction off our wardrobes and wear burlap sacks? Definitely not. The "burlap sack look" is not exactly a bridge to love and connection with others. But it does mean our goal is not to be the cutest girl in the room. It means the purpose of our appearance is not to hide our imperfections. It means being honest about our vanity so that we can scale it back a step or two. It means that when we go to a social event or coffee or dinner, the last thing our friends need is for us to be competing with them or raising the bar for them to jump even higher.

It also means reframing our physical imperfections as opportunities. When I look back on that interaction with the woman at the store, I see it so differently now. At the time it happened, I behaved as if my appearance was about me, which is why I wanted to hide. I apologized to her for how I looked, but I wasn't really thinking about her at all.

If I could do it all over again, I would have a different perspective. I would see it as an opportunity to throw a wrench in the gears of the comparison machine. Even if that woman looked at me and thought, "Whoa, Sharon is a hot mess!" that isn't necessarily a bad thing. Because you know what she wouldn't be thinking? She wouldn't be thinking, "Sharon *always* looks put together, even at

7:00 a.m. I can never measure up to her." Between the two options, I choose the first, because that is a gift. Whenever we relinquish our splendor, we fight back against the impossible standards for women. When we lower the bar for women around us, expose our weaknesses instead of "keeping up," and humble ourselves instead of competing, that is a gift to our sisters. In an image-obsessed culture like ours, that's what love looks like.

Missional Image

Humbling ourselves as an act of love is an audacious way to reclaim our appearance, but it's not the only way. Returning to Paul's strategy of being "all things to all people," appearance is something to steward. Both Paul and Jesus remind us that appearance is a point of connection, which should inspire us to be intentional about it. For me personally, whether I speak to a group of women or simply attend a dinner party, I want to be relatable. That doesn't mean hiding my identity or overhauling the way I dress, but it does mean having a posture of love. In the back of my mind, I try to consider whether my appearance will encourage relationship or distract from it; is it a bridge to the gospel or a barrier?

Stewarding one's appearance is going to look different for different people, and that's a good thing. We need different examples of living this thing called faith, and each of us connects with different styles. That's why legalism has no place here. We don't have to judge other people on the way they dress simply because it's different from us. Instead, we can focus on the purpose of our own appearance, because there is incredible freedom there. God can use everything about us—inside and out—to draw people to him, and the more we lean into that mission, the greater peace we will find. In contrast, when we make our images about us, there is only ever striving. There will always be more commercials identifying new flaws, more online tutorials teaching us how to improve our hair. But when we root our images in mission, it gets us off the hamster wheel and sets our feet on rock.

It might seem like a small thing, or a vain thing, to give so much attention to your appearance, but as theologian Abraham Kuyper famously put it, "There is not a square inch in the whole domain of our human existence over which Christ, who is Sovereign over all, does not cry, Mine!"[7] Every single bit of you, from the tips of your toes to the depths of your soul, was created with purpose, and that purpose is to love.

Focus Verse

"[Christ] made himself nothing by taking the very nature of a servant, being made in human likeness. And being found in appearance as a man, he humbled himself."—Philippians 2:7–8

Focus Prayer

Lord, I confess I am tempted to focus on appearance. Vanity is a constant pull, and too often I put my self-image above love for others. Set me free from this focus, which hurts me and the people around me. Teach me to follow your Son, who humbled his appearance as an act of love for you and for us. And change my heart, so that I don't humble myself begrudgingly, but gladly. Amen.

Discussion Questions

1. Have you ever apologized for your appearance (or even the appearance of your home)? Why do we do this?
2. When you look at the people around you (your friends, family, neighbors), what do you perceive to be some of their biggest struggles with appearance?

3. In your own life, what might it look like to humble your appearance? What can you scale back on?

4. Humbling your appearance can be hard. What are some of the fears and hesitancies that spring to mind when you think about taking these steps?

5. How can we overcome our fears and reluctance to humble our appearance?

Six

When You Make Your Possessions about You

Vanity costs money, labor, horses, men, women, health and peace, and is still nothing at last.[1]

—Ralph Waldo Emerson

rowing up, my family had everything we needed—more than we needed, really—which means there was a lot I took for granted. We lived in a big brick house with towering white columns and a "terrace" (not a porch) in the back. I attended a private school where the students were privileged and everything we had was brand-new. When I turned sixteen my parents bought me a brand-new Honda Civic, and I'm embarrassed to admit I was disappointed. All my other friends had received SUVs, so I thought I was being "deprived."

I was supremely sheltered, and probably a little annoying too, because I was so completely out of touch. I hardly understood anything about the world, never having to sacrifice, budget, or save because I always had everything I needed. I also assumed most families lived like mine, which makes me laugh to think back on. It wasn't until I left that world that I realized how privileged I was.

Today I am the wife of a pastor. We have more than we need and we live comfortably, but my life is more modest than it was. I would love to say I have handled the transition with grace, but I haven't. One evening we were reviewing our family's finances, figuring out what else to cut back. Through gritted teeth I put "new clothes" and "home décor" on the financial chopping block, because we didn't really *need* those things. Our house doesn't *need* curtains, and the boys' rooms don't *need* to be painted. I don't *need* the newest, trendiest shoes. Those luxuries could wait until we had more margin, so we cut them out.

Of course, cutting those things off the list was the easy part. The next day I noticed a pair of boots at the store, and boots are, ironically, my Achilles' heel. They were a pair of taupe suede chunky-heeled booties, and everything inside me wanted to try them on. But what was the use? There was no money to buy them. So I stood there in the store silently willing them to be mine, until I gave up and pouted away. I'm telling you, it *hurt me* to leave those boots behind.

Some of you are reading this and thinking, "Get a grip, woman," and you know what? You're totally right. Those boots were not that big of a deal. But some of you are right there with me. You know exactly how I felt. For some of you, buying clothes or decorations for your home is your therapy. It's what you do when you're stressed or sad or having a bad day. New clothes are your pick-me-up, and a cute home gives you confidence. That was my emotional crutch too.

When we no longer had the financial margin for my "therapy," I had to examine my relationship with things. Until then, I had never been forced to face my dependence on possessions, but in the last decade I have confronted the idol head-on. I have done some deep heart work detangling my identity from what I own, and I've learned a lot about myself.

One of my big realizations is that for me, it's not just about having nice things. I do appreciate a high-quality blouse or a well-made piece of furniture, but my possessions are also about much more than that. I want people to know I have good taste. I don't want people to come into my home and think, "Ohhh, Sharon does *not* know how to decorate." I feel the same way about my clothes: I want to look like I know what I'm doing. In my home and in my life, I want to look put together.

Take the story of the blue plates.

Before we moved into our current house, we temporarily lived in an apartment, and almost all our belongings were in storage. To save us the time of unpacking and repacking our things, my parents bought us temporary plates, silverware, and cups. It was an incredibly generous gift, but there was a small hitch: my dad bought them. He handpicked our dishes with incredible charity, but with not a care for my dining room "aesthetic." All of that to say, I wouldn't have chosen the ones he chose. The dishes were all made out of thick, navy blue plastic. They were totally functional, and totally ugly.

It's such a vain thing, but I hated those plates. I hated them with the fire of a thousand suns. I hated how they made my loveliest meals look gross, and how they didn't match a single thing I owned. But what I hated most of all was when other people saw them. Whenever we had guests, I apologized for the plates (notice a pattern?), as if the sight of them was offensive. "I'm so sorry we have to eat on these plates," I began. "These aren't our plates. They're just temporary. Our own plates don't look anything like this!" As if our friends cared about them *at all*. One of our friends literally laughed in my face and said, "I don't think I've ever heard anyone apologize for plates before." I should have listened to what he was saying, but he was a man, so I ignored him. Of course he didn't get it. Most men don't care about plates.

In reality, he was doing me a favor. He was giving me a glimpse into my friends' priorities, which were not plates. They cared about spending time with me, while I, on the other hand, remained preoccupied with my appearance. I couldn't stand the thought of looking anything less than perfect, a perfect hostess with a perfect home. I wanted people to know those plates were not acceptable to me. Never in a million years would I pick them out, and *people needed to know that*.

Looking back, this story epitomizes one of two ways we make our possessions about us. There are, of course, many ways we develop an unhealthy dependence on our things, which is why Jesus spoke so often about them (Matt. 6:19–24; Luke 6:24–25; 12:15, 33–34; 16). It's tempting to trust in our possessions and to seek safety and security in them. However, there are two specific ways we make our possessions *about us*, as if to communicate "Look at me" or "Look at what I have," and they are **vanity** and **greed**.

Vanity

One of the biblical passages that gets to the heart of vanity—and also one of the most misunderstood passages in Scripture—is 1 Timothy 2:9–10. In these verses, Paul gives the following instructions to women:

> *I also want the women to dress modestly, with decency and propriety, adorning themselves, not with elaborate hairstyles or gold or pearls or expensive clothes, but with good deeds, appropriate for women who profess to worship God.*

Merriam-Webster defines *modesty* as "the freedom from vanity." However, modern teachings on modesty sometimes miss this definition, focusing instead on covering women's bodies. What a lot of people don't know is that this passage is a caricature of wealthy women of the day.[2] Paul wasn't as concerned with women's hemlines as he was their extravagance. He was discouraging them from flaunting their status.

This context is important, because some of the most popular teachings about modesty—which focus on sexual modesty—can miss the principle underneath it. The truth is, modesty is about much more than covering up. These verses appear within a larger context about worship, which means Paul had one priority in view: God's glory. He was urging men and women to pursue a modesty by which their glory was decreased and God's was increased. In that sense, modesty is about the orientation of our heart—our hearts should be oriented toward God's glory instead of our own—and this principle lays claim to everything in our lives.

The truth is, we can cover every inch of our bodies without addressing immodesty in our hearts. If our basic desire is still for attention and glory, then modesty is not in us. Nineteenth-century British writer Anna Jameson went so far as to say, "Extreme vanity sometimes hides under the garb of ultra modesty."[3] Even our fair trade purchases, which meet the highest standards of ethics and human dignity, can be placed in service to our image. As good and important as fair trade is, we have to guard against using these products to look like a "particular kind of Christian." That's how subtle and sinister vanity can be. It doesn't always present itself as extravagance. It can take the appearance of humility and generosity too, or as Thomas Aquinas put it, we can pass off our sins "under the aspect of good."[4]

There is no cure-all for rooting out vanity, because it assumes so many forms. For some it might mean simplifying your lifestyle. For others it might mean using your possessions to bless others.

Or it might mean spending less effort presenting a certain "image" on social media, even if that image is a good one. For all of us, our one hope is that God would grant us eyes to see it. Humans have a marvelous capacity to deceive ourselves, which is why the psalmist prayed, "Search me, O God, and know my heart! Try me and know my thoughts! And see if there be any grievous way in me" (139:23–24 ESV). When prosperity is the status quo, we need the eyes to see it.

Greed

The second way we make our possessions about us is **greed**. The difference between vanity and greed is that vanity serves our status; it's fundamentally about our glory. Greed, on the other hand, has a much smaller aim, which is satisfied merely by *having*. Greed comes from the insatiable belief that "if I can just have THAT, *then* I will be happy." As W. Jay Wood, a philosophy professor at Wheaton College, described it, "Greed is an inappropriate attitude toward things of value, built on the mistaken judgment that my well-being is tied to the sum of my possessions."[5]

In a materialistic culture like ours, it's important to understand why our possessions don't satisfy us. German psychologist Erich Fromm explained it well when he said, "Greed is a bottomless pit which exhausts the person in an endless effort to satisfy the need without ever reaching satisfaction."[6] Fromm was not a Christian, but he understood something essential about the human soul. Even though we are finite creatures, we bear the image of an infinite God, which means we cannot be satisfied, quenched, or contented by anything smaller than the breadth and depth of our souls. Even the most extravagant possession is like a drop of rain in the Grand Canyon: it cannot fill the massive emptiness, or even begin to. And our souls are the same. We cannot be filled by anything short of God.

Jesus affirmed this spiritual truth when he spoke to the woman at the well: "Everyone who drinks this water will be thirsty again, but whoever drinks the water I give them will **never thirst**" (John 4:13–14, emphasis mine). What Jesus is saying is that nothing on earth can provide the contentment we crave. Not the big house, not the leather boots, not the promotion at work, not the fast car. None of these things can guarantee satisfaction. The promise is a lie.

Greed, then, is not about what you have, but what you desire and why. When you pine after a bigger home, a better car, nicer clothes, or more money, simply because they would make your life "better," that is the handiwork of greed. Whether or not you have those things is irrelevant to whether or not greed is in your heart.

Does the sin of greed mean we shouldn't enjoy our possessions? Not necessarily. In 1 Timothy 6:17, Paul makes this distinction clear:

> *Command those who are rich in this present world not to be arrogant nor to put their hope in wealth, which is so uncertain, but to put their hope in God, who richly provides us with everything for our enjoyment.*

"Hope in wealth" is the definition of greed, which Paul contrasts with "hope in God," but he also makes clear that this world is "for our enjoyment." The answer to greed is not poverty, but priority. The source of our contentment and hope should never be our things, but our God.

I speak that truth to myself a lot. There is a neighborhood adjacent to ours full of beautiful, sprawling mansions, and whenever I drive past them, the ache of discontentment drums louder. In those moments, I remind myself of this truth: the people living in those homes are not guaranteed anything I don't already have access to myself. Their possessions can't promise them joy or peace. And neither can mine. As Jesus himself put it, "The peace I give is a gift the world cannot give" (John 14:27 NLT).

Created to Give

The root word of "vanity," *vanus*, means "empty," which is the perfect word picture for both vanity and greed. When we make our possessions about us, we attempt to fill a void inside us, but we enlarge the void instead. It's a strange paradox, but the more we use our things to fill us, the emptier we become.

I want you to linger on that point for a moment, because God doesn't warn us against greed solely because of how it affects others. Vanity and greed are bad for the world and bad for our witness as the people of God, but they're also bad for us. When we make our stuff about us, our souls shrivel and crumple in on themselves. It's one of the fastest shortcuts to discontentment and a life of striving. Vanity is, in fact, painful. We give that pain labels like "envy" and "comparison"—and many times, it is—but the cause of the pain, at its core, is a false hope in things.

God has an answer to the pain of vanity. Rather than rebuke our misplaced hope, he points us to a better way. The word *give* appears over one hundred times in the Gospels alone: "Give to the one who asks" (Matt. 5:42); "freely give" (Matt. 10:8); "sell everything you have and give it to the poor" (Mark 10:21); "Give, and it will be given to you" (Luke 6:38); "Give glory to God" (John 9:24). Jesus was constantly talking about giving, but he also walked the walk. Most scriptural references to "giving" are about God and what he has given to us. As Paul David Tripp put it, "The Gospel is the ultimate generosity story captured by the words, 'God so loved the world that he gave . . .'"[7]

God is a giver, and we are made in his image, which means our calling is to give. Generosity is at the heart of the Christian life, and it's our answer to the pain and emptiness of vanity and greed.

In a culture of consumerism, it also makes us a subversive group. Generosity is one of the ways we distinguish ourselves from the world. We are to be the ones constantly looking for ways to give, to bless, to loosen our grip on our possessions. We cannot be content to look at our things and passively remind ourselves, "I shouldn't love them too much." That mind-set has zero accountability and is discernible to no one. The only way to bear witness to the Giver, and the only way to prevent our possessions from possessing us, is to develop a habit of generosity.

Throughout the Old Testament, the Israelites were commanded to give the "firstfruits" of their harvest (Exod. 23; Num. 18; Prov. 3), and this command is a great paradigm for thinking about giving. The "firstfruits" were the first produce of a harvest, gathered and offered to God before the farmer knew the extent of his yield. He didn't know if his harvest was plentiful or sparse, whether he was giving out of surplus or scarcity. He simply gave in obedience and trust.[8] I was recently challenged by this truth, because most of us give out of our surplus. We give the leftovers, or an amount that doesn't affect the way we live. But giving the firstfruits means giving in complete faith. It means giving in ways that don't make sense, that require trust, and that influence our standard of living. This is the kind of radical generosity to which we are called, and with a cheerful heart (2 Cor. 9:7).

I don't think this means we must all take a vow of poverty. Like I said, the world has been given to us to enjoy, and the principle of firstfruits implies the possession of a harvest. What I do think it means is that generosity is an important check on our hearts. It keeps us spiritually healthy. It keeps our priorities in line. It keeps us dependent on God instead of our things. It reminds us that our stuff is not about us, and it's an essential way to honor God and love others.

I once heard a financial planner warn against buying the cheapest house in a neighborhood, or living in a high-income community. She explained her logic this way:

Psychologically that's a bad strategy. If you have the cheapest, smallest house on the block, you're looking up. You're looking at people with more income than you. You're setting your consumption standards to your neighbors. And if you have a little bit of envy or anxiety that you're not catching up with your neighbors, you are going to overspend.[9]

This advice is a complete reversal of my assumptions. My tendency is to focus on people who have more than I do in order to make myself feel humble. *Look how much I'm sacrificing*, I self-righteously gloat. In reality, when you focus on those who have more, you are far more tempted to envy. You can't help but compare yourself to the people just ahead of you. That envy shapes your financial choices, but more importantly, it makes generosity harder.

Once again, this is the power of focus. Vision determines direction. If our eyes are fixed on those with more, our hearts and lifestyles will follow. Conversely, the financial planner explained, when we look to those with less, our hearts are encouraged toward modesty, gratitude, and generosity.

The financial advisor wasn't speaking from a Christian perspective, but we can take her principle one step further. In addition to focusing on those with less, we can also focus on him who made himself less. Philippians 2 tells us that Jesus "did not count equality with God a thing to be grasped" but took "the form of a servant" (vv. 6–7 ESV). This is the God version of moving into a lower-income neighborhood, and we were created to imitate him.

That financial advisor didn't know just how right she was. As Christians, we are called to focus on the lowly—on the Savior who lowered himself and on the poor he came to save—and that focus will determine our direction. It will also give weight to our witness. In a world held captive to consumerism, vanity, and greed, we are the people of the Giver. We point to the God who loves and gives and has enough for all by embodying that generosity with our lives. In a world where millions of people are hungry and homeless and wondering if God even cares, our mission couldn't be clearer. Gandhi is rumored to have once said, "There are people in the world so hungry, that God cannot appear to them except in the form of bread." Jesus, the bread of life, invites us to embody his generosity. What we have is not ours but belongs to a much bigger story.

Focus Verse

"Command them to do good, to be rich in good deeds, and to be generous and willing to share. In this way they will lay up treasure for themselves as a firm foundation for the coming age, so that they may take hold of the life that is truly life."—1 Timothy 6:18–19

Focus Prayer

Lord Jesus, it is so easy to find security and confidence in my possessions. And it is tempting to fear their loss. Too often, I live as if you are a God of scarcity instead of a God of abundance. Help me to trust your character, and to bear witness to it with my priorities and my lifestyle. Set me free from greed and vanity, and give me a generous heart. Amen.

Discussion Questions

1. Prior to reading this chapter, how would you have defined *modesty*? How would you define it now?
2. Why is it so tempting to put our hope in "things"?

3. Which "things" are you most tempted to place your hope in, or to turn to for comfort and relief?
4. What makes you hesitant to be generous?
5. What would it look like to give the "firstfruits" of what you have?

Seven

When You Make Your Friendships about You

It is best to consider anyone a friend who drives us closer to God.[1]

—Ann Voskamp

*I*t was the first week of high school and I was standing in front of my locker, adjusting my backpack and about to attend the next class. Just as I shut the door and headed toward the sidewalk, one of my friends approached me to chat. We talked for a minute or two and then, out of nowhere, she asked, "Do you pluck your eyebrows?"

Pluck my eyebrows? I thought to myself. I had never even heard of such a thing. It sounded barbaric and totally unnecessary. Why would someone do that to themselves? Why would *I*?

"No . . ." I replied, curious but cautious. Where was she going with this?

"Why do you ask?" I prodded, foolishly taking the bait.

"Because you're supposed to have two eyebrows. Not one."

And with that, it all became clear: this girl was not on a mission of love, saving the world one unibrow at a time. No, this was a sneak attack, teen girl guerilla warfare, and I had just been ambushed.

Throughout the twenty years since, this story has continued to make me laugh. It was so diabolical it could have come straight out of the *Mean Girls* "Burn Book." I didn't have a unibrow, but she had probably heard the line somewhere and was carrying it around like ammunition.

Teenagers can be brutal, which is why most of us have stories like this from our past. It's common. What is less common—or should I say, less *expected*—is when this dynamic inhabits our adult relationships. Some of the worst friendship drama I have experienced has occurred during my adult years. And some of the most painful wounds I have ever experienced have come from my adult friends.

I was not prepared for this part of adulthood. There are plenty of books about mother wounds, father wounds, and wounds from an ex, but there aren't as many resources for friend wounds. Perhaps it's because friends seem safer, as if we are less vulnerable to them somehow, and that's what makes the pain so shocking. Betrayal, rejection, and misunderstandings between friends don't just hurt; they surprise you with how much they hurt. It's like a sucker punch. You don't see it coming.

As much as these wounds hurt me and jarred me, they also uncovered an unhealthy reliance on my friends. Like most relationships, it's easy to make our friends "about us," to turn them into mirrors of our self-worth. The way they treat us, or how we perceive them to be treating us, can seem like a value judgment on us as people. The size of this influence becomes especially clear when a friendship fails or a close friend betrays us. It's not that these heartaches shouldn't sting—Jesus himself was hurt by his friends—but how we respond to them reveals a lot about our hearts, and even reveals our idols. How do your broken friendships shape your self-image and influence your thought life? How you answer that question says a lot about whether your friends are functioning as mirrors.

With that in mind, I want to focus on two forms of friendship brokenness that shape our self-image. The first is perhaps the most obvious: **rejection.** Rejection is so tempting to make "about us," so we'll look at how it influences self-esteem and how to respond to it. The second brokenness we will look at is a little different: **loneliness.** Loneliness does not always result from a friendship ending, but the inability to make close friends. Loneliness can still reveal an inordinate emphasis on the mirror of friendship, so we're going to look at its effects, as well as what God says about it.

Rejection

Throughout my twenties I experienced romantic breakups and friendship breakups, and it's difficult to say which was harder. After a few of my friendships fell apart, I just about fell apart myself. There were times I was so devastated I could hardly eat because the pain was so crushing.

Not all friend rejections are so dramatic and devastating. There is the friend who doesn't return your text messages, the friend who forgets your birthday, or the friend who ignores you at church. In the past, my default was to assume these interactions were all about me, and that I had done something wrong. In reality, it was almost never about me. My friend was simply distracted, or busy, or she had a family emergency. The "snub" was not a rejection at all, but instead a sign that *she* needed love and care. That's what happens when our friends are just mirrors reflecting on us: perceived rejections magnify our own insecurity, and consequently blind us to the needs of others.

One of the most common types of rejection is feeling left out, which results from both intentional and unintentional rejections. While my husband and I were living in the Chicago area, I was desperate to make friends, so I put myself out there again and again. One afternoon I was on the phone with a new friend, talking about our plans for the weekend. She asked if I was going to a party at a mutual friend's home, and I wasn't. I hadn't been invited. The conversation moved on and I tried to play it off, but I felt like I had been kicked in the stomach. As soon as I hung up the phone I broke down sobbing. Under ordinary circumstances, the exclusion would have only stung, but I was exhausted from trying to make new friends. I wondered why I hadn't been invited and what I possibly could have done wrong. Was I not likable enough? Fun? Interesting? Relatable? What was wrong with me?

These types of slights—both the big ones and the small—are common, but can still be the source of great anguish. Maybe you weren't invited to a book club, a Bible study group, or that elite circle of co-workers, and it's hard to shake it off. Especially when social media is covered with photos of smiling faces from the event, minus your own.

These wounds can take a hefty toll on our self-esteem, but they have a second downside as well: they draw our focus inward. Rejection asks, "Why not me?" which launches us into a spiral of introspection about our personal defects. When that happens—when we assume the rejection is about us—we fail to ask a much more important question: "Why not her?" or "Why not him?"

One of the lies behind the question "Why not me?" is that *I alone was excluded*, and that's exactly what Satan wants us to believe. He wants us to think we're alone, that *everyone* was included except us, or that there is something particularly objectionable about us.

96

Of course, this is a lie. About 90 percent of the time, it's not personal. Most likely we weren't singled out to be excluded. Most likely it had nothing to do with us at all, which we can easily diagnose by asking, "Why not her?" What other names are missing from the list? What other faces are not in the photo? When you take the time to ask this question, you begin to notice numerous people—great, fun, lovely people—who weren't invited either. Whatever the situation, the question "Why not her?" or "Why not him?" jolts us out of our self-pity so that we can see the other people who might feel excluded too. The more we have that kind of vision, the less we are consumed by the question "Why not me?"

That is also what Jesus did. Jesus constantly gave his attention to the rejected and the people on the margins. Throughout the gospels, the disciples argued about who was most important, who was most "in," and each time, Jesus directed their attention to those outside the group—the servants, the children—and said, "Be like them." He was always looking after the people who got left out, the very people we ignore when we ourselves are rejected.

But what if the rejection *is* personal? What then? First, it is always a healthy exercise to take any personal responsibility we can. Proverbs 27:6 tells us, "Wounds from a friend can be trusted," which means we shouldn't always dismiss them out of hand. Sometimes there is something in the wound we need to see and embrace. If, however, the rejection is totally unjustified, Jesus is our nearest comforter. When we are rejected, we join the company of a Savior who was rejected too. Jesus felt this brokenness more acutely than anyone, and he knows our pain. Jesus also did more than relate to our rejection; he redeemed it. Jesus entered into the brokenness so that rejection would not be the end of our story. Instead, God uses our exclusion to grow us. Somehow, on the margins, God does a work in us that he would not have done had we been included. Somehow, in that place of feeling left out or rejected, God makes us more like him.

That's why I no longer wish away my rejection, but am learning to embrace the redemption. When I feel overlooked or ignored, I ask God what he wants me to learn from it. Sometimes he is humbling me. Sometimes he is giving me a heart for the rejected. Sometimes he is helping me die to myself. And sometimes he is pruning something toxic in my soul. But if I simply wish away the heartache, I wish away redemption too.

When we make rejection about us, it's hard to see God's redemptive work because we can't see past ourselves. Our focus is so thoroughly inward, that we don't see the plans he has for our pain. But as Romans 8:28 reminds all of us who love him, God always has good plans.

Loneliness

You have already read a piece of my story of loneliness in Chicago. What I haven't told you yet is how long that loneliness lasted. Two years after we relocated, I still had very few friends. Over time, the loneliness became a source of insecurity, which added even more pressure to the process of making friends. Whenever a potential friend came along, I behaved like a drowning swimmer grasping for a raft. Desperate for attention but not wanting to appear needy, I coached myself to "be funny, but chill," which sounds so sad to admit out loud. But that's where I was, and it wasn't long before the loudest voice in my head was shouting, *There must be a reason this is so hard. Maybe I just don't fit in here. Maybe everyone has all the friends they need—why would they bother making time for me?*

During that season, I happened upon an article titled "The Lethality of Loneliness." The article was about the science of loneliness, and it helped me understand why the lack of female community felt like an open wound. The article drew a distinction between "loneliness" and "being alone," since many of us feel lonely in spite of having friends. Loneliness, it explained, comes from the lack of *close* friends. Even when you're surrounded by people, loneliness is "the want of intimacy." The author added that loneliness is not just painful, but it can be hazardous to our health. She writes,

> Long-lasting loneliness not only makes you sick; it can kill you. Emotional isolation is ranked as high a risk factor for mortality as smoking. A partial list of the physical diseases thought to be caused or exacerbated by loneliness would include Alzheimer's, obesity, diabetes, high blood pressure, heart disease, neurodegenerative diseases, and even cancer—tumors can metastasize faster in lonely people.[2]

In contrast with the negative consequences of loneliness, studies have found that female bonding is good for your health. Research shows that when women spend time with other women, it counters the effects of stress on a biological level. During quality time together, a woman's body releases a hormone called oxytocin, "which enhances relaxation, reduces fearfulness, and decreases the stress responses typical to the fight-or-flight response."[3]

This information was a revelation for me, because it validated how I was feeling. These scientific findings meant that I wasn't pathetic or weak when I felt lonely. That ache was the voice of my soul communicating its need. God created me for community, and loneliness happened when I was out of sync with that intended design. It's true for me, and it's true for everyone on earth. We are meant for human connection.

Science aside, God gave community a high priority by making it an integral part of his story. Since the beginning of creation, God made us to live in relationship, declaring, "It is not good that the man should be alone" (Gen. 2:18 ESV). We often assume this verse is about marriage, but it's about much more than that. Genesis 2:18 is the blueprint for all of humanity, meaning it is "not good" for any of us to be alone. That's why God's entire story, from beginning to end, always involves a "people." Whether he was addressing Israel or addressing the church, community was a basic part of his plan. Community, along with the Holy Spirit, is how we follow Jesus, and it's how we flourish as human beings.

All of that to say, loneliness is not a sign that something is wrong with us. It means something is wrong with the world. Loneliness is a sign that things aren't what they should be, and that there is a gap between reality and intention. It is strangely good news that loneliness isn't "about us," and it can keep us from becoming paralyzed. The temptation of loneliness is to stop trying, because building community is such hard work, and many of us reach a point of throwing in the towel.

When we reach that point of throwing up our hands and calling it quits, that's exactly what the enemy wants. He wants us to turn our loneliness into self-imposed isolation, so that it becomes its own self-fulfilling prophecy: *Why bother forming community? People don't want to be my friend anyway.* That is the lie loneliness whispers, and we have to reject it. God desires us to be in community, even when it's slow to come.

My season of loneliness didn't last forever. It took a few years, but we made some amazing friends in Chicago. When we finally moved back to North Carolina, it was just as gut-wrenching as it had been to leave. Ike and I knew we would miss our friends, and we wept over the distance. Those friendships were a lifeline during a difficult time, and we will be forever grateful for them. But I'm grateful for the loneliness too. Through it, God was making me into something new.

The God Who Calls Us "Friend"

We used to sing a song in church called "I Am a Friend of God." Maybe you've heard it, and maybe you even like it, but boy oh boy,

I did not. I actively disliked this song. I had no legitimate reason for my scorn, such as a problem with its theology or its message; I just didn't like it. It didn't speak to me. The words sounded cheesy, and it seemed too informal for the Creator of the universe. God isn't, like, my buddy.

What I didn't realize at the time, and what might have improved my attitude, is that Jesus claimed this description for himself. In John 15 he refers to his disciples as his "friends," and in verse 13 he describes the kind of friendship he is offering: "Greater love has no one than this: to lay down one's life for one's friends." With these words, Jesus proclaims his life and death the definitive act of friendship.

When we look at "Jesus the friend," what do we see? First, we see a perfect friend who loved, forgave, and endured with his friends, but still experienced rejection. His friends abandoned him and betrayed him at his time of greatest need. Then, Jesus endured the ultimate loneliness of being forsaken by God.

Jesus knew the pain of broken relationships better than anyone, and that is a great comfort for those who follow him. But it's also a challenge. Jesus's example calls us out of the pity parties and paralysis of broken friendships. Rather than languish in rejection, God challenges us to become ministers of reconciliation (see 2 Cor. 5:18), a calling that transforms us as we go. That is probably one of the biggest changes God has accomplished in me. Because of my own experience, I am a new kind of comforter. These days, I get fierce over lonely and rejected people. I reach out to them the way I wish others had reached out to me. I am patient with their insecurity and their pain, the way I wish others had been patient with me. I do this because I get it. I know how much it hurts. I've been there. I won't stand by and watch others go through it alone.

This, I believe, is how God works. He takes our exclusion and makes us more like him. He takes our broken friendships and transforms us into better friends. As Lysa TerKeurst puts it in her book *Uninvited*, "being set aside is actually God's call . . . to be set apart."[4] On the heels of rejection, there is mission.

David and Jonathan, Ruth and Naomi, Mary and Elizabeth, Jesus and John. Each one of these friendships testifies to how powerful, good, and important friendship can be. Our best friendships sharpen us and strengthen us. They call us toward our higher selves. They are God's provision in executing his mission on earth. But friendships make for a terrible mirror. Friendships are *for* us, but they are not *about* us. They exist primarily for the glory of God. They point us toward the perfect friendship we have with him, and as long as our friendships remain grounded in that truth, even the broken ones will be swept up into the arc of redemption.

Focus Verse

"Greater love has no one than this: to lay down one's life for one's friends."—John 15:13

Focus Prayer

Jesus, you are the perfect friend. You never reject me. You never abandon me to loneliness. Instead, you took on rejection and you took on abandonment in my place. You laid yourself down for me in the ultimate act of friendship, and I thank you and praise you for it. Teach me to be a friend like you. Help me to see my friendships as a part of my mission on earth, rather than a reflection of myself. And thank you for doing it first. Amen.

Discussion Questions

1. How has rejection or loneliness shaped your self-image?
2. Why are we so quick to assume that snubs are about us?

3. In what ways has God used your wounds to make you a better friend?

4. How can we discern between unjust rejection and "wounds from a friend," which we should welcome?

5. Based on Jesus's example, what does it mean to be a good friend to someone?

eight

When You Make Your Calling about You

Work is . . . the full expression of the worker's faculties, the thing in which he finds spiritual, mental and bodily satisfaction, and the medium in which he offers himself to God.[1]

—Dorothy Sayers

When I was in high school, I thought I would grow up to become a psychologist. I had always wanted to help people, and counseling seemed like a great option. My psychology teacher affirmed my aspirations, and at the end of my senior year I won the Psychology Award. In hindsight, the "Psychology Award" strikes me as a strange award to receive, but at the time, I took it as a *word from the Lord*. I was called.

I left for college with a lot of certainty about my future. I would major in psychology and that was that. So I signed up for Developmental Psychology and began the work of fulfilling my destiny. I was ready to step into my calling.

That is, until the day I discovered something terrible.

What I didn't realize until halfway through the semester is that psychology involves more than listening to people and helping them. If you want to major in psychology, you also have to do math. And statistics. And research. Honestly, I might have been able to stomach the research, but math is the place my soul goes to die. I was out. I struggled the rest of the semester, and Developmental Psych was my worst grade of the year.

As it turns out, I was not called to psychology.

Outside of class, I was becoming more involved with Fellowship of Christian Athletes. My faith was growing like it never had before, and my passion for God was bursting at the seams. I loved learning about Jesus and I loved my community of friends. That season of my life was like a spiritual rebirth, and it was then that I discerned a call to ministry.

Although my calling was clear, it took awhile to figure out the shape of my call. After college I spent a year working for Proverbs 31 Ministries and learning the ropes of women's ministry. Then I went to seminary. Then I worked as a college minister. Then I went back to seminary. Somewhere in there I began blogging. It was something I enjoyed and felt gifted in, so I kept at it year after year. Over time, I realized writing *was* my ministry, and my ministry was growing. Not by leaps and bounds, but slowly and surely. I was getting more opportunities to write, and I was meeting other writers like myself. My writing improved and my love for it bloomed, and I began to dream bigger dreams.

In the beginning, I started writing because I felt called. Writing was my sweet spot, the place where my gifts and my passions met, which was satisfaction enough. I wrote because I couldn't *not* write. But over time, something inside me shifted. My heart began to need more than the ministry itself. Instead of simply enjoying my calling, I began to crave affirmation in it. Without positive feedback, my confidence was fragile.

My calling had become about me. Ministry, a calling that is foundationally about God, had become a servant to my own success and my pride. It's not that I didn't care about God, or that I wasn't concerned with his glory—but I was more concerned with my own.

I share this story because it illuminates something true for all of us. If I can make *ministry* about me, then no calling is immune. Even the best, noblest, and humblest callings are vulnerable to self-focus. Whether you're a CEO, a social worker, or a stay-at-home mom, your calling can become about you. And when it does, it will shrivel your soul like a flower scorched by the sun.

When we look at the stories in Scripture, we see two major consequences of making our callings about us: dissatisfaction and disobedience. The first knocked me flat on my back for the last several years. The second has affected me in subtler yet significant ways.

Dissatisfaction

About three years ago, I reached a breaking point. I had been writing and teaching for nearly seven years, but I wasn't enjoying it anymore. In fact, it had started to hurt. It's not that I was overworked or burned out—I wasn't—but I felt ready for more, and God wasn't providing it. My ministry felt small and invisible, and somehow that invisibility had weight. I was a small fish in a sea of writers just like me, and the comparison was crushing me.

In the middle of that season, I attended a conference feeling desperate for a word from God. I needed some sort of direction, some sort of help to climb out of the pit of my own insecurity. As luck would have it, I happened to sit with two women I looked up to. Both were writers, both were teachers, and both were wise women of God. At the first chance I had, I unloaded my mess. Wild-eyed and thirsty for wisdom, I gripped the table between us and leaned in. I pleaded with them for some shred of advice.

Both women were silent for a number of seconds, and then one of them answered me plainly:

"Your ministry, your writing, your calling—it can't be about you."

She was right. Exactly right. But I wasn't ready to grasp what she was saying. It wasn't until a month or two later, when I heard an interview between authors Christine Caine and Jennie Allen, that I heard the words that would finally sink in:

> People are trying to build their platform more than their charac-
> ter. . . . I've spent more time thinking how I can die a thousand
> deaths so that the character and nature of Christ can be formed
> in me. As I die more, God gives me greater influence. I think what
> we have is a generation that doesn't want to die, but wants to have
> a bigger voice.[2]

That was it. That's what I had been doing. I didn't want the obscurity or the invisibility or the toil without success. I wanted to be known and celebrated. Affirmation was the only reward that mattered to me, and without that reward, I couldn't be satisfied. I couldn't enjoy my calling. All this time, I had seen my smallness and invisibility as obstacles standing in my way, when in reality, they *were* the way. God was calling me into a season of obscurity for my own sake. Just like Caine said, God was using my smallness to deal with my character and prune my heart. But I didn't want it, because I couldn't see God's hand. I only saw failure.

That is the first major consequence of making our calling about us. In his book *Courage and Calling*, Gordon Smith explains that when we make our calling about us, what we get is a "false satisfaction."[3] In other words, your successes only provide you with a fleeting joy. If your calling is a personal measuring stick, then your self-esteem will depend on the day. Did you make the deal? Did you get the promotion? Did your recipe turn out right? Were your sales numbers up? Did you get into the program? Did you get through the day without screaming at your kids? Did anyone see you, affirm you, or validate you? Each one of these successes or failures can influence your contentment and your self-worth, which is the power and the danger of making your calling about you. The satisfaction of self-focused calling drips through our fingers like oil. That was what happened to me, and it was painful—but God did something so interesting with my pain.

As much as it hurt, my dissatisfaction was a mercy. It was a severe mercy, but a mercy nonetheless. That's because my pain and discontentment were a taste of the life I thought I wanted. God was letting me taste its fruits, just a bit, so that I would develop a *distaste* for it. He was letting me experience how miserable it is to make my calling about me, so that I would stop and turn back before I went any further.

And it worked. I became so sick of writing and teaching for my own reputation and glory, so eaten up by comparison and insecurity, that I quit. I didn't stop writing, but I did retreat from the temptations toward self-focus. I scaled back my time on social media, I stopped keeping track of my readership, and I took a forty-day fast from my blog. I gave myself the time and space to pray, heal, and get my priorities in line. I surrounded myself with people who would encourage me to focus on Christ instead of competition. And slowly, my joy returned.

Dissatisfaction is a torment, but it's also a teacher. It reveals our false idols, and it forecasts our future. It's a cautionary tale of the life we think we want, and in that sense, it's a grace. God is beckoning us, oh so lovingly, away from false satisfaction and into satisfaction that is true.

Disobedience

In 2011, about five years after I began writing, I started contributing to a new blog for women called *Her.meneutics*. Under the umbrella of *Christianity Today*, it spotlighted the voices of women. I appreciated the site because it was doing something unusual. It wasn't simply featuring the voices of women; it featured deep, theological perspectives from women. The writing was both relatable and smart, and I loved it.

Do you know what I didn't love? The comments section. Although many of the comments were supportive and encouraging, some of them were downright mean. I was called all sorts of names by people who didn't know me at all, for reasons that weren't even clear. Eventually I decided to stop reading the comments, but they had already gotten inside me. Especially when it came to my boldness. As I already shared, I loved to be seen as the "good Christian girl," and I had always thought my writing served that image. But that's not how the commenters saw it. They thought I was "stupid" and "dangerous." They disagreed with my ideas and called me names. I wasn't a good Christian girl to them.

It didn't take long before I began altering my voice. I avoided writing on hard topics, and I stuck to safe, uplifting, positive messages that were likely to receive the least pushback. Instead of speaking the truth in love, I bent to fear.

That is the second pitfall of me-centered callings. At some point, a self-centered calling conflicts with God-centered callings, because God-centered callings always lead to a cross. God-centered callings involve suffering, sacrifice, and looking like a fool, because this is the path of the Savior we follow. If your calling is about your image, or your reputation, or your comfort and convenience, it will eventually diverge from the path of Christ. At some point, God will ask you to do something that isn't about you, or doesn't feel good, or requires you to suffer, and you will have to make a choice.

When we reach that intersection, the me-centered calling tempts us toward disobedience, and that's what happened to me. I stopped writing the way God called me to write. I stayed safe and covered my tail, writing messages I thought people wanted, instead of the messages they probably needed. That's what happens when your calling is all about you, and the resulting disobedience takes an endless number of forms. There's the Christian businessman who hedges on his ethics to get ahead. There's the evangelist who uses his God-given charisma to prey on the vulnerable and indulge his greed. There's the parent who doesn't want to be the "bad guy" and fails to enforce healthy boundaries for their kids. Whenever your calling is about you, your reputation, your comfort, or your success, disobedience is not far behind.

Of course, "calling" refers to more than a career. Throughout his letters, Paul describes the calling of every Christian "into fellowship with his Son" (1 Cor. 1:9), to "live in the grace of Christ" (Gal. 1:6), "to be free" (Gal. 5:13), and to live "a holy life" (2 Tim. 1:9). All believers everywhere are "called" to these things, which means "calling" also refers to the Christian life. Each of us is called to follow Jesus.

Yet even in this, we can make the Christian life about us, and it manifests in a subtle but "acceptable" form of disobedience. For many of us, we treat Jesus and the church as a means to a more comfortable and sheltered life. It is so tempting to construct a world in which our schools are Christian, our music is Christian, our companies are Christian, and our only friends are Christian. We clump together in our Christian corners, where we don't have to interact with anyone who is unlike us, anyone who comes from a different background, and we call it community. But really, it's an escape. It's also not the calling we as the church have received.

In the face of this self-serving form of discipleship, Jesus's life stands in stark relief. His call is less comfortable, wholesome, and safe than it is risky and revolutionary. He promises sacrifice, not comfort. He leads us into the homes of prostitutes and tax collectors, and all the way to the cross. Jesus's life is a scandalous alternative to sentimental notions of the gospel. Does that mean the safety of our kids doesn't matter? Definitely not. Are all of us called to be martyrs? No. But the call of Christ does check our assumptions and our priorities. If wholesome and safe is our compass, then we will always choose convenience over obedience.

The good news is that, while Jesus doesn't promise us wholesome and safe, he does promise freedom, abundance, and peace. If we have the courage to follow him and trust him for that, then that's our inheritance. We can put down safe and pick up satisfied. Put down comfort and pick up contentment. Obedience demands endurance and grit, but its fruit is life.

Christ-Centered Calling

Remember the story of Paul's contentment in Philippians? The one I could hardly believe? There is something else I didn't mention before, which makes his testimony even more amazing. While Paul was under house arrest, monitored by Roman guards and facing an uncertain future, things got worse. He caught wind of a group of fellow Christians who were preaching Christ out of envy, "supposing that they can stir up trouble for me while I am in chains" (1:17). These people were, in theory, on Paul's team. They should have had his back. Instead, they behaved like rivals. They viewed Paul's imprisonment as a victory in a competition they never should have been playing.

It's hard to imagine how that must have felt. At a time when Paul desperately needed support, he was betrayed by people *in the name of* Christ. Had I been in Paul's position, I would have despaired. I would have become bitter, and I would have lost hope in the church.

But that's not what Paul did. Instead he said,

111

But what does it matter? The important thing is that in every way, whether from false motives or true, Christ is preached. And because of this I rejoice. (1:18)

I will never get over that response. Never. The betrayal rolls off Paul like water off a duck's back. But how? Why didn't it bother him? Why didn't he give up on Christians and abandon organized religion? The reason he didn't cave in to cynicism is that his ministry was never about the approval of others. He wasn't living for them or himself or his reputation. He was singularly focused on the glory of God, and nothing else mattered nearly as much. This focus rescued him from hate and despair.

Philippians is a portrait of a man who is free because he wasn't weighed down by the burden of self. He wasn't living for his glory, so nothing was on the line. He wasted no time defending himself or his motives, because it didn't matter. That wasn't the point. And because of that, he was free.

That's what Paul is getting at in Philippians 4:11–12 when he says this:

I have learned to be content whatever the circumstances. I know what it is to be in need, and I know what it is to have plenty. I have learned the secret of being content in any and every situation, whether well fed or hungry, whether living in plenty or in want.

Paul was content in all things because his calling was not about him. His job was not about him, and his life was not about him. It was all about Jesus. Paul was a living, breathing example of Jesus's words that his "burden is light" (Matt. 11:30). When your self-worth is no longer on the line, the weight is infinitely less.

That's why we fight to keep our focus on God. No matter how or where God calls us, our focus will drift inward and we've got to fight that pull. When we have nothing to prove and nothing at stake but Christ alone, we experience the lightness our souls crave.

There is also another reason to fight the pull. Christ-centered calling is the best way to love the people around us. When I altered my writing in order to be liked, I was, ironically, not loving my readers at all. I wasn't giving them Spirit-inspired words. I wasn't giving them the messages they needed to hear. I was only serving myself. In his book *Every Good Endeavor*, Tim Keller writes, "Our daily work can be a calling only if it is reconceived as God's assignment to serve others."[4] That's the beauty of God's order: when we love him, we love others too. One inspires the other. So for the sake of God's glory, for the sake of others, and for the sake of your very own soul, guard your focus. Remember what your calling is for. It's not about you, and that is great news.

Focus Verse

"Whatever you do, work at it with all your heart, as working for the Lord, not for human masters, since you know that you will receive an inheritance from the Lord as a reward. It is the Lord Christ you are serving."—Colossians 3:23–24

Focus Prayer

Loving Father, I confess I am tempted to make my calling about me. I find my identity and my worth in my successes and my failures, and it steals your glory while robbing me of my joy. Lord, I want to be free of this cycle. I want to pursue you and only you, and to enjoy the freedom it brings. Whenever I feel insecure or small, help me to identify the idols behind those feelings, and root them out. I want to live and serve for you alone. Amen.

Discussion Questions

1. What is God calling you to in this season of your life?
2. In what ways are you tempted to make your calling about you?
3. What have been the consequences of making your calling about you? (How does it make you feel? How does it affect your relationships? How does it influence your obedience?)
4. How can you think of your calling in a more Christ-centered way, one that lightens your burden?

nine

When You Make Your Church about You

The purpose of the worship service is not what we get out of it but the God who has drawn us into it.[1]

—Jared Wilson

I should probably begin this chapter by apologizing to every worship pastor I have ever had. When it comes to music, my pickiness rivals that of an eight-year-old at a seafood buffet. My husband can bear witness to my agonized sighs during the songs I dislike. It is extremely rude, and I am the worst. When I get to heaven, I will be the person tapping God on the shoulder, asking if we can sing more hymns.

I hate to admit this tendency in myself, but I also know I am not alone. Most church members are like me. We all have our "thing"—some aspect of the church that is important to us and which we are especially sensitive to. For me, it's the music. If the songs seem too human-focused, or too repetitive, or the theology seems shallow, or the quality of the music is bad, I whine about it. I can't tell you how many Sunday afternoons have been spent dissecting the music. I even do this at churches where I love the worship and the worship pastor.

For some of you, your "thing" is totally different. It could be the preaching style, the sermon content, the programs, the service times, the lack of young people, the lack of older people, the friendliness of the pastors, or how available the leaders are to meet with you one-on-one. We've all got a thing (or multiple things), and it almost singlehandedly determines the level of our contentment at a church.

When I first set out to write this book, I didn't plan to include a chapter on church. It simply wasn't on my radar. Then one morning—ironically, during the church service—I realized something. My attitude about church music, and the church in general, is deeply self-centered. Occasionally my complaints are about the essentials, but most of them are purely preferential, and I am a master at framing my preferences as essentials.

On more occasions than I care to admit, I have treated my church like it's all about me, and as I already mentioned, this mentality is not uncommon. Many of us view the church through a critical, me-centered lens, because we live in a culture shaped by consumerism. Our society is all about choice and customization. When we go to the store, we can choose between eight different kinds of mayonnaise. When we shop for clothing, there are endless racks of outfits to sort through. When we go to Starbucks, we can order a drink with six different steps. And how about choosing a restaurant? I don't know if you have this problem, but it takes my husband and me *days* to pick a place. There are so many options in our area that we go back and forth and back and forth, trying to settle on the perfect spot. Eventually the choices become paralyzing.

This consumer mentality shapes the way we buy groceries, houses, and cars, but it also shapes the way we choose a church. It's a mentality addressed by author Skye Jethani in his book *The Divine Commodity*. In it, Jethani explains how consumerism has seeped into the church:

> Through the influence of our consumer culture, with its emphasis on immediate gratification, combined with our innate selfishness, many of us approach church the same way. . . . We make calculated decisions about which community will offer the most comfortable environment, and our commitment to that group lasts only as long as the comfort endures.[2]

Jethani adds, "In Consumer Christianity, our concern is not primarily whether people are transformed to reflect the counter-cultural values of God's kingdom, but whether they are satisfied."[3]

This is a pretty strong indictment of Christians, but I do think it's fair. In fact, I don't have to look hard to recognize the tendency in myself. I was raised in the church and I know what commitment "should" look like, but whenever relationships get hard or my church isn't meeting my preferences, I pine for the church down the street. I daydream about their amazing worship, their contagious outreach, or their cutting-edge women's ministry. I wonder how it might be better—or easier—if I was there.

So I get it. I understand the consumer mentality. But when we make church about us, we can expect two outcomes: shallow friendships and a shallow faith.

Shallow Friendships

I won't spend much time on this since I wrote an entire chapter on friendship, but for a brief moment I want to reflect on this truth: friendships take time.[4] My best friends are the ones who have walked beside me through thick and thin. The best small groups

I have belonged to were forged through years of weekly meetings, group dates, and family potlucks. None of those relationships would have been possible without long-term, intentional presence in one another's lives.

Because friendships take time, it's impossible to establish solid relationships when we hop from church to church. In fact, it's a special kind of irony when Christians roam from church to church, dissatisfied with each one's community. The best communities cannot form that way.

That said, making friends as an adult is hard. It can be lonely and frustrating and emotionally draining. When you're a single person surrounded by married people, or an older person surrounded by young families, it can be alienating and painful. In the midst of this tension, Jesus offers understanding and a way forward. Jesus spent every day with the same twelve men, and only one of them is described as a "beloved" friend (John 21:20). That's not to say he wasn't close to the others, but I suspect he had different levels of connection with them. After all, few of these men understood anything Jesus was saying. They misinterpreted his teachings and missed the point of his ministry. They asked selfish questions and competed with each other. So you better believe Jesus got annoyed with them. They were, after all, a bunch of smelly dudes. I'm sure some snored or told bad jokes, and I would bet money that one of them had a weird laugh. They all had human foibles, like humans do, which might be the reason Jesus needed time away (Luke 5:16).

Despite all that, the men he chose are the men he remained committed to and even died to save. In turn, each one of the disciples eventually died for him. It is a full-circle sacrifice with a powerful message: by being a good friend to the disciples, Jesus turned the disciples into good friends.

When friendship is hard or inconvenient, that is the story we recite, because it points to something essential about Christian community. One of the reasons our friendships are shallow is that we approach them with the same consumer mentality. We want instant gratification, and when we don't get it, we move on.

Jesus, on the other hand, had a different approach. Rather than gather men who immediately "got him," he waited for the connection to come. In the meantime, he was a good friend. He took the lead, set the standard, and waited with patience. Over time, the disciples grew into intimate friends, and that model of friendship is a basic function of the church. Our call is not to gravitate toward people like us but to gather strangers and turn them into family. To gather enemies and turn them into friends.

In Matthew 5:46–47, Jesus says,

> *If you love those who love you, what reward will you get? Are not even the tax collectors doing that?* **And if you greet only your own people, what are you doing more than others?** *Do not even pagans do that?* (emphasis mine)

Worldly friendship takes the path of least resistance. In worldly friendships, similar individuals clump together in cliques of "their own people." Jesus, on the other hand, shows us a different vision of friendship. Rather than gravitate toward people like us, we press in toward people who are different. As C. S. Lewis put it in his book *The Four Loves*, "Friendship is not a reward for our discrimination and good taste in finding one another out. It is the instrument by which God reveals to each the beauties of all the others."[5] This is, in fact, some of the most important work of God's people. God calls us to build the bridges that no one else will build. He calls us to overcome barriers no one else will overcome. Our friendships should be so radical, so illogical, so unlike anything else we see in the world, that we are known for them.[6]

When the church is about Jesus instead of ourselves, it calls us into those uncomfortable relationships. Yes, it's hard. Yes, it's frustrating. But it is our witness to a world that is afraid of differences. It's our example to a world yearning for authentic demonstrations of love.

Deep friendships are good for us. They provide us comfort in hard times, hope when we're tempted to despair, accountability when we stumble, and encouragement in our faith. We need friends to help us become the people God created us to be, which brings me to the second consequence of making church about us: shallow faith.

Shallow Faith

Several years ago, actress Gwyneth Paltrow made headlines when she announced that she and her husband, musician Chris Martin, had decided to end their marriage. The news was controversial because of their approach: they had rejected the term "divorce," and were instead describing their separation as a "conscious uncoupling."

To explain this terminology, Paltrow shared a post on her website written by doctors Habib Sadeghi and Sherry Sami. In the post, Sadeghi and Sami made the case that modern marriage is outdated. The concept of lifelong marriage, they argued, originated when human life expectancy was much shorter. Now, humans live much longer, and the average marriage cannot withstand the evolution of each spouse. As a part of their argument, the authors drew an analogy between marriage and an insect's exoskeleton. Insects with exoskeletons are attached to an outer shell that keeps them "stuck in a rigid, unchanging form that provides no flexibility."[7] This, Sadeghi and Sami believed, is a lot like the current form of marriage: it's too rigid and inhibits our growth.

Not long after Paltrow made this announcement, my friend Jennifer Grant wrote a gentle response for *Her.meneutics*. Jennifer had a number of disagreements with the concept of conscious uncoupling, but there is one I will never forget. Responding to the insect analogy, Jennifer wrote,

> I believe marriage is a sacrament, an outward sign of divine grace. **Living out that sacrament and engaging in real forgiveness is what keeps my husband and I from becoming rigid, hollow people**—not trading our spouse in when we feel bored or disappointed or not "happy" anymore.[8]

I love that description of marriage, because it highlights marriage's essential purpose: God designed marriage to make us more like Christ. In good seasons and bad, the marriage relationship grows us and deepens us, if we let it. The more we lean into that design, even when it's frustrating or exasperating, the more God transforms us into his likeness. In fact, the hardest parts of marriage can also be the holiest. The "obstacles" are actually opportunities to grow, as long as we don't retreat from them.

Why am I talking about Gwyneth Paltrow and marriage in a chapter about the church? Because that is how I think about church membership. I take my commitment to church very seriously, almost as seriously as marital vows. That might sound strange in a culture like ours, but when I commit, I am all-in. It's the only way it will work. No marriage works if you run when things get hard. If your marriage exists solely to make you happy, it won't last. And it's the same with the church. If happiness is your primary requirement, you won't stay long.

The second reason church is similar to marriage is that both are designed to grow us. They grow us when things are good, but especially when things are bad. Learning to be in community with people who are different, learning to trust imperfect leaders, learning to listen to people with whom you disagree, learning to forgive and reconcile with people who hurt you—this is all the work of the church. It's all the stuff of a deep and lasting faith, but we miss out on it if we leave at the first sign of trouble.

121

The truth is, some of the hardest, most uncomfortable parts of church are good for our souls, and we can cling to that truth. When we are disappointed or frustrated or we don't understand a decision, we can ask God what he is teaching us. What blind spot is he trying to reveal? How can this situation grow us? Those moments have incredible power to transform us, if we're open to them.

Is there ever a time to leave a church? Yes. Definitely. Sometimes staying only enables a toxic situation. But I believe the antidote to consumerism in the church is the same antidote to consumerism in marriage. We commit to both for the long haul, not because they ultimately make us happy, but because they make us holy.[9]

An Attitude of Gratitude

Dietrich Bonhoeffer was a famous Christian martyr who died resisting the Nazi regime. At a time when German Christians were largely silent about Hitler's rise to power, Bonhoeffer was a dissenting voice. He helped lead the "Confessing Church," which was the only Christian movement openly opposed to Hitler. Because of its stance, the Confessing Church was deemed illegal by the Nazis, so Bonhoeffer spent several years teaching seminary underground. It was during this time that he lived in an intentional community of Christians and wrote a tiny book called *Life Together*.

Life Together explores the gifts and challenges of living in Christian community. Even though it was written over seventy-five years ago and under circumstances quite different from ours today, the similarities between Christians then and now are remarkable. Bonhoeffer's community wasn't plagued by consumerism, but it did have many of the same struggles we have, because it had the same sin. Sin corrupted the church the way it corrupts the church now: by undermining unity. Whether we live in a consumer culture or not, sin divides, and unity is something we will always have to fight for.

In one prophetic passage, Bonhoeffer foreshadows the consumer mentality, warning against looking for an "ideal" church:

> Those who love their dream of a Christian community more than the Christian community itself become destroyers of that Christian community even though their personal intentions may be ever so honest, earnest, and sacrificial.[10]

With these words, Bonhoeffer cuts to the core of our best intentions. Even when our desires for the church are noble, good, and right, we have to guard our attitudes closely. A critical spirit is an easy entry point for sin to sow seeds of division. Bonhoeffer observed this firsthand, watching Christians become "proud and pretentious" because they were always comparing the reality to the ideal. When the reality fell short, they became "accusers" of both the leadership and the members.

Years later, Christians still struggle with this. We have to reconcile our "ideal" church with the reality of our options. For Bonhoeffer, the solution to this problem was simple: gratitude. He writes, "We enter into that life together with other Christians, not as those who make demands, but as those who thankfully receive."[11] I love this perspective, not only because it reverses the spirit of criticism but because it springs from a central Christian teaching, which is that we need each other. The body of Christ is diverse, full of different people with different roles, and according to Scripture, every role matters. In 1 Corinthians 12:12–27, Paul explains that every person is a necessary member of the body of Christ, and if a single part is missing or unable to contribute, the entire body is weaker for it.

In other words, we cannot be who God created us to be, and we cannot serve the way he created us to serve, without each other. When we're frustrated with our church, or our pastor, or fellow members, Scripture encourages us instead to thank God for one another and to appreciate the roles we play in one another's lives.

This attitude of gratitude also directs our focus to the Giver. When we pause to thank God for his church, we remember what church is ultimately about, which is not us. God created the church, he is in control, and he has a long history of using terrifically imperfect people to do incredible things. No church is below that redemptive grace, so we don't have to be indignant on God's behalf. He knew what the church would be like, he knew the mistakes it would make, and he chose her anyway.

I once heard someone say they would only give up on the church when Jesus did. That perspective was so convicting to me. Our perfect Savior has a hopelessly imperfect bride, and I contribute to that imperfection every day. But God is faithful still. His faithfulness to me and his people leaves me without excuse. If I claim to follow him, I must follow him in this. Some days are harder than others, but here's the good news: the church may not be *about* us but it is *for* us. God did not intend for us to follow him by ourselves. We are meant to do life together, in a support system of people who love us, sharpen us, and grow us. This beautiful community is one of the many benefits of making Jesus the center of church. The fruits are vast and rich, even when we don't like the music.

Focus Verse

"And let us consider how we may spur one another on toward love and good deeds, not giving up meeting together, as some are in the habit of doing, but encouraging one another."—Hebrews 10:24–25

Focus Prayer

Lord, you know that we are a broken people, and brokenness breeds brokenness when we come together in community. That is what makes the church so hard sometimes, but that is also why you died for her. Help me commit to love and

*serve the church with the same fierce faithfulness as you.
Open my eyes to the aspects of church that I make about
me, and use those hard places to grow me in the likeness of
your Son. Amen.*

Discussion Questions

1. What is your "thing" at church, the thing you are super picky and opinionated about?
2. How have you dealt with your "thing" poorly, or well?
3. What might God be teaching you, or changing in you, through the parts of church that frustrate you?
4. God gave us the church as a help and a gift. In what ways have you been blessed by the church? What are you grateful for about the church?

Interlude

y mom has a 1909 Steinway grand piano, and this piano is like nothing you've ever seen. The piano is made out of rich marbled mahogany in an elegant Victorian style. The frame is garnished with perfectly carved curls and swirls, and the piano stands on tapered Corinthian columns. The whole instrument is a work of art, and its appearance is only matched by its sound.

Like all pianos, this one requires a lot of maintenance. Growing up, I remember a man coming to our house twice a year to tune it. One by one, he tapped the keys while tightening and loosening the strings. It was a long process, but I loved hearing each note tiptoe and then thunder, as he drummed the keys with various amounts of force.

Years later, my husband and I lived in a house with another Steinway piano. We were both students at the time, and we had the great luck of living in a large home as caretakers for the owner. The living room had a high ceiling with a wall made entirely of glass, and beside the wall stood a classic black grand piano.

We never learned much about the piano, but judging by its authentic ivory keys, we guessed it was at least seventy years old.

The piano was not nearly as ornate as my mom's, but it was still a priceless antique. When I slid onto the bench and pressed my fingers against the keys, it was like traveling to a different era. I could practically hear the music and the clicking heels of party-goers doing the Charleston.

There was only one problem: the owner hadn't maintained it. Whenever you pressed a key, the sound came out warbled and off pitch. If you tried playing "Jingle Bells," it sounded like "Christmas in the Haunted Mansion." The instrument was gorgeous, but it had an awful sound.

Those two Steinways had similar origins. They were made out of the finest materials by the most skilled experts. They were built to be the best. However, their quality wasn't fixed. They both re-quired lifelong maintenance to preserve their excellence. Without care, these instruments could not do what they were created to do.

That's the thing about musical instruments. Left untouched, instruments drift. No matter the materials or the craftsmanship, they have to be retuned again and again.

The human soul is a lot like that. It drifts. Without deliberate retuning, it goes out of tune with the gospel. This tendency was first described by an ancient bishop named Augustine, who no-ticed his own soul "drifting." He discovered that apart from the grace of God, our souls turn inward on themselves. We become bent. Salvation unbends our souls and points us toward God and others, but left unchecked, our souls will always drift back to that inward position.[1]

Put another way, self-focus is not a temptation of the few but a human default. Our focus is constantly pulled inward, which means we have to guard our hearts and minds. We have to tune and retune our souls to Christ, or else we'll bend right back again.

Focusing on God and others is easier said than done, especially when human nature works against us. If we could snap our fingers and make the change, we would all be selfless people in no time flat.

But the truth is, our souls don't work that way. There is no trick or shortcut. Self-forgetfulness requires ongoing discipline. Retuning.

After I grasped the importance of self-forgetfulness, I spent the following years figuring out how to embody it. What needs to happen in our lives to stop making everything about us, and make it about God instead?

God has been walking me through that answer, and I'm eager to pass along the lessons I learned. In the following chapters we'll look at four different ways to be "free of me": praise, people, purpose, and passion. Each one of these habits has been freedom for me, so I can't wait to share them with you.

Before we dive in, I want you to know that this list is not exhaustive. Instead, I'm giving you four broad categories for resisting self-focus. I hope you will treat these as a jumping-off point to go even deeper, because this is just the tip of the iceberg. Two resources that might also help you are Richard Foster's *Celebration of Discipline* and Dallas Willard's *The Spirit of the Disciplines*. These books explain practices like prayer, fasting, confession, silence, frugality, and even secrecy (which means to "abstain from causing our good deeds and qualities to be known"[2]), all of which give handles to the principles in this section. They will take you even further down the path to freedom in simple, practical ways.

And of course, none of this unbending is possible without the help of the Holy Spirit. We cannot will ourselves to focus on God any more than a blind person can will themself to see. God must heal us first. It all begins with him, so ask God to set you free from the smallness and powerlessness of self-focus. It's a request God promises to fulfill, because 1 John 5:14 assures us, "This is the confidence we have in approaching God: that if we ask anything according to his will, he hears us." It is God's will for us to live and breathe for him, so put down the burden of doing these practices on your own, and simply ask.

PART 3

How to Be Free of Me

ten

Praise

Why Loving God Sets Us Free

We can't cure our narcissism by trying to ignore ourselves.
The solution is to stare at God.[1]

—Francis Chan

The name of my blog is *She Worships*, and it sometimes confuses people. I didn't anticipate this when I named the site ten years ago, but several times a year someone says to me, "I visited your blog expecting it to be about music." Worship, after all, is what we call our Sunday mornings. We walk into a church building and sing our songs, which are usually led by a "worship pastor." That, in a lot of people's minds, is worship.

When I originally named my blog, I had something different in mind. In Romans 12:1–2, Paul tells us to offer ourselves as living sacrifices, and that is our "true and proper worship." The term "living sacrifice" always stood out to me, because it's such a strange thing to say. In Paul's context, the term "sacrifice" would have conjured images of spotless lambs and unblemished goats, offered at the temple to God. The Israelites gave their firstfruits and their best livestock as a sign of God's ultimate priority. To make a sacrifice was to make a declaration of trust in God. It was a tangible sign of belief in his provision and his value. A sacrifice signified that God was worth more than anything we might possess. To the Israelites, that was sacrifice.

A "living" sacrifice, then, is the human embodiment of those things. It's a lifestyle that demonstrates our confidence in God, as well as his priority in our lives. The word *worship* literally means "to ascribe worth," so Paul was saying, "You are a living testimony of God's worth. Everything you do points to his glory." In *The Message*, Eugene Peterson renders the verses this way: "Take your everyday, ordinary life—your sleeping, eating, going-to-work, and walking-around life—and place it before God as an offering . . . fix your attention on God." Colossians 3:23 elaborates on this idea even more: "Whatever you do, work at it with all your heart, as working for the Lord, not for human masters." Worship, then, is the substance of the Christian life. It's not a Sunday morning affair, but something daily and rather ordinary. No matter what we do, no matter how small, it all belongs to the higher work of praising God.

What I didn't realize until recently is that worship isn't simply our purpose. It isn't just a good thing to do or a godly thing to do. It's also our help. Worship awakens us, heals us, and rescues us. Worship is part of God's plan for our salvation. In my season of wilderness and self-doubt, worship was my deliverance. It was my ladder out of the pit, my refuge, and my joy.

And this is how.

Stop the Train

When I first realized that self-focus was fueling my insecurities, I started paying attention to the moments when it raged. There were some days when my insecurities were more painful than others, and I wanted to understand why. Why couldn't I let go of that mean comment online? Why was I so affected by a misunderstanding with a friend? What was going on inside me when my insecurities took the reins? After doing some internal investigation, this is what I learned:

Whenever I experienced rejection, obscurity, invisibility, exclusion, failure, or disappointment, something very specific happened: my mind spiraled out of control. My thoughts raced with questions like "What's wrong with me?" and "Why am I not good enough?" and "What could I have done differently?" In other words, the wounds didn't simply fuel my insecurity, but my self-focus too. And all the positive self-talk in the world didn't help.

Eventually, with the help of our marriage counselor, I was able to give a name to this downward spiral. Our counselor explained that there are times when our thoughts spin out of control. They practically take on a life of their own, feeding on each other and gaining power. When this happens, when our train of thought goes off the rails, we have to intervene. We have to **stop the train**.

What I needed was a way to derail the locomotive of self-focus. But how?

I spent a lot of time praying and thinking about how to hit the brakes on my train of thought whenever insecurity and self-focus took the wheel. I decided that the opposite of self-focus was to focus on God, so I designed a little experiment. Every time I noticed myself getting carried away, every time the pain of rejection or invisibility sent me into a flurry of me-centered thoughts, I actively stopped myself and turned my thoughts to God. I focused on who he is, and I praised him.

That's how I stopped the train of thought, by cutting off its fuel supply. Whenever my insecurities geared up and all those "me" thoughts flooded in, I ran to a list of God's attributes and recited them again and again:

- The Lord is wise (1 Cor. 1:30; James 3:17)
- He is faithful (Deut. 7:9; 2 Thess. 3:3; 2 Tim. 2:13)
- He is holy (Ps. 22:3; Isa. 6:3)
- He is gracious and compassionate (2 Kings 13:23; Ps. 145:8; Joel 2:13)
- He is merciful (Luke 6:36; Eph. 2:4)
- He is just (Deut. 32:4; Isa. 30:18)
- He is slow to anger and abounding in love (Exod. 34:6; Num. 14:18; Neh. 9:17)
- He is our strong tower (Ps. 61:3)
- He is our rock (2 Sam. 22:32; Ps. 18:2)
- He is our refuge (Ps. 46:1; 91:2)
- He is great in power (Nahum 1:3)
- He is a Savior (2 Sam. 22:47; Luke 1:47)
- He is a redeemer (Ps. 78:35; Isa. 47:4)
- He is a fortress and a hiding place (Ps. 32:7; 144:2)
- He is good (Ps. 34:8; 100:5)
- He is patient (2 Pet. 3:9)
- He is kind (Ps. 69:16; Titus 3:4)

The list could go on and on. Scripture is full of descriptions about God, and I loved combing through books like the Psalms to find new truths I could cling to. Whenever my insecurities kicked in, I recited the list until my heart rate slowed and my breathing calmed down. In short, I praised my way out of it.

And let me tell you, this practice has literally changed my life. It has stopped the train dead in its tracks. At first it took some practice, because my brain was used to turning inward. I would begin to praise God and, moments later, my thoughts would be back in the muck. But the more I did it, the easier it became. It shifted my focus off of my pain and onto the One who heals.

The Power of Praise

On a purely practical level, this habit is effective at getting your mind off of yourself. However, a part of me wondered if I was simply distracting myself. By shifting my focus off of my insecurities and onto God, was I merely avoiding the problem? Was this an unhealthy form of escape? The Christian equivalent of therapy shopping?

No. There is a key difference between the worship of God and superficial distractions. One is an escape, the other a return. One avoids what's going on inside of you, the other restores you.

In his book *Reflections on the Psalms*, C. S. Lewis wrestles with the entire purpose of praise. He admits he stumbled over the notion of a God who clamors for praise "like a vain woman wanting compliments."[2] In a moment of clarity—and comedy—Lewis realized that "even if such an absurd Deity could be conceived, He would hardly come to *us*, the lowest of rational creatures, to gratify His appetite. I don't want my dog to bark approval of my books."[3] Lewis continued to explore the nature and purpose of praise, which led him to this epiphany:

> I had never noticed that all enjoyment spontaneously overflows into praise. . . . The world rings with praise—lovers praising their mistresses, readers their favourite poet, walkers praising the countryside, players praising their favourite game—praise of weather, wines, dishes, actors, motors, horses, colleges, countries, historical personages, children, flowers. . . . The Psalmists in telling everyone to praise God are doing what all men do when they speak of what they care about.[4]

Lewis then concludes:

> I think we delight to praise what we enjoy because **the praise not merely expresses but completes the enjoyment.** It is its appointed consummation.[5]

What Lewis is saying here is that there is no greater joy than praising praiseworthy things. It is the reason you tell people about your child's achievement in school, the reason you recommend that restaurant you love, and the reason you gush about the incredible band you discovered. It is also the reason why it's hard to keep joy to yourself. I can't tell you how hard it was for my mom to keep the news of my pregnancies a secret. She nearly burst! That's because good news begs to be shared.

The opposite of praise-inspired joy is self-focused insecurity. Picture your mind as it swirls with self-doubt, the questions about why she snubbed you, why your spouse is in such a bad mood, why no one gave you credit for your work, why your friends didn't call. Consider how you feel in those moments. The pit in your stomach, the sour taste in your mouth, the pain in your heart. It's an awful feeling, but that is what self-focus does. It's the difference between a spirit of joy and the gall of insecurity. That's not to say you shouldn't feel hurt, but how you respond to the hurt is a step toward one or the other.

That's why we can embrace the truth that God created us to praise. And the more praiseworthy the thing, the more joy we have in praising it, a principle that finds its ultimacy in God. "Joy," John Piper wrote, "is not a mere option alongside worship. It is an essential component of worship."[6]

That's also why my "strategy of praise" is more than a distraction or an escape. It's what we were created to do. We were created to worship. It's why we exist. When we take the time to meditate on God and praise him for who he is, our souls connect with their God-given design, and we see this all over Scripture. Think of Mary, who could have responded to the news of her pregnancy with fear or anxiety or disobedience. Any one of those responses would have been understandable. Instead, she praises God (Luke 1:46–55). Or there's Job, who loses his family and every earthly possession, and his first action is to worship God (1:20). There are Paul and Silas in Acts 16, who sing hymns to God in prison (v. 25). Or Leah in Genesis 29, who finally realizes that the only balm for her husband's rejection is not to have more children but to worship. Over and over, people praise God not in spite of their difficult circumstances but because of them. In the kingdom of God, worship is not an illogical choice but the only choice. It is our help, our hope, and our joy.

Praising God also restores our sense of proportion. In her book *Humble Roots*, Hannah Anderson explains, "Pride confuses our identity with God's and makes us think of ourselves as larger than we really are."[7] That's what self-focus does. The more we focus on ourselves, the bigger we will seem, and the greater a burden we become to ourselves. When we focus on God—his vast power and might, his unsearchable and unknowable ways—we realize our smallness. It's like standing on a mountain or beside the ocean. In that moment, you discover your true proportion. You feel small in comparison with the cosmos, and there is a beautiful lightness in that realization. You are tiny. You are fragile. You are not in control. The world does not rest on your shoulders, and that is good news. There is so much relief in accepting our smallness, and praising God takes us to that place.

No one explains this principle better than theologian John Stott, who put it like this:

> If worship is right because God is worthy of it, it is also the best of all antidotes to our own self-centredness, the most effective way to "disinfect us of egotism," as one writer put it long ago. In true worship we turn the searchlight of our mind and heart upon God and temporarily forget about our troublesome and usually intrusive selves. We marvel at the beauties and intricacies of God's creation. We "survey the wondrous cross on which the Prince of glory died." We are taken up with God, the Father, the Son and the Holy Spirit. . . . Because we are normally so turned in on ourselves, we will not find this easy. But we have to persevere, since nothing is more right or more important.[8]

Praising God is about more than stopping the train. It's about being who God created us to be and doing what God created us to do. Yes, it takes our focus off ourselves and places it on God, but it goes deeper than that. This strategy works because it's not simply a strategy. It's our purpose in life.

The Baader-Meinhof Phenomenon

A few years ago I learned of a concept called the Baader-Meinhof Phenomenon.[9] The term was invented by Arnold Zwicky in 1996, and it refers to an experience you have probably had. Have you ever learned a new word, or heard about a new book, and then all of a sudden, you noticed it everywhere? My most recent memory of this phenomenon was with the word *draconian*. I read it online, then heard it on the radio, and then a friend of mine used it in a sentence, all within the span of a week or two. It was so strange, because who uses the word *draconian*? (Not me!) Now that you have read this, you will probably hear it tomorrow. And if you do, that is the Baader-Meinhof Phenomenon.

I also experienced this phenomenon after I began searching Scripture for references to worship, praise, and meditating on God's Word, especially as they related to abundant life. Soon, I was finding them everywhere. The Psalms, for example, are full of this theme (emphasis mine):

> *I will meditate on your precepts and **fix my eyes on your ways**.* (Ps. 119:15 ESV)

> *Then I shall not be put to shame, having **my eyes fixed on all your commandments**.* (Ps. 119:6 ESV)

> *My soul is consumed with **longing for your laws** at all times.* (Ps. 119:20)

140

Blessed is the one . . . whose delight is in the law of the LORD, *and who* **meditates on his law** *day and night. That person is like a tree planted by streams of water.* (Ps. 1:1–3)

I will consider all your works and **meditate on all your mighty deeds.** (Ps. 77:12)

I will walk about in freedom, for I have **sought out your precepts.** (Ps. 119:45)

In Psalm 119 alone, the word *praise* appears six times, and the word *meditate* appears six times. Over and over, the psalmist makes a connection between fixing our eyes on God and his Word, and the pursuit of abundant life. Meditating on God and his truth is not just a nice thing to do. It is the way to freedom.

After discovering this pattern in Scripture, I began reading God's Word with new eyes. For most of my life, I understood the commands to meditate on God's Word as a "good Christian thing to do." Of course we should meditate on Scripture. That's Christianity 101. What I didn't understand then, and what I do understand now, is that these commands are not checklists. They are lifelines. The Scripture writers meditate on God's Word because it is their rescue. It is an essential piece of God's saving grace. When the writers declare that God is their refuge, his Word is one of the ways we access it. When our minds spiral out of control with lies and fears, the truth of God is our safe haven. Praising God and remembering his attributes *is* our deliverance. And that truth is everywhere in Scripture.

As I already mentioned, this discipline has changed my life. It has also given me a new, revolutionary understanding of worship. If I could choose my legacy, it would be reclaiming the true meaning of worship, which is power and freedom and hope for the worshiper. Worship is not a once-a-week deal, but an entire way of life. God invites us to worship him in all we do, not because he is vain but because he is good. When we praise God, it nourishes us. It gives us healing and peace. That's not to say that praising God always feels good and natural, or that it comes easily. Sometimes I recite my list of attributes with a reluctant heart and a stiff upper lip, taking it as medicine for my soul. But over time, through this discipline, God has set me free from "me." Worship has taken the power out of my insecurities and self-absorption, because now I know what to do with them. Whenever my focus shifts toward myself, and heartache naturally follows, I now know where to turn. I praise him.

As a final thought, I would be remiss if I left you thinking worship is a solitary affair. Praise in the midst of pain is not solely about self-talking the gospel. Instead, worship belongs in the context of community, because the truth is, some days we can't bring ourselves to do it. It's too hard. The darkness is too heavy and the grief too close. In those moments, when we can't turn our thoughts to anything besides grief and our voice is too hoarse from wailing, we need brothers and sisters to worship on our behalf. We need a church home where we can go and sit, surrounded by proclamations of truth and hymns of worship. We need a community to name the lies and rebuke the enemy and preach the gospel to us. That is why the story of God has always been a story of a people. Worship is not something "you" do alone, but something "we" are meant to do together.

Focus Verse

"I keep my eyes always on the LORD. With him at my right hand, I will not be shaken."—Psalm 16:8

Focus Prayer

Heavenly Father, gazing on you is life itself. I was meant to do it. You created me for it, and I want to step into the fullness of my design. Teach me how to be a creature of worship whose reflex is to praise you, even when life presses in. Teach me to worship, even when it doesn't make sense, for the sake of my soul and the power of your glory. Amen.

Discussion Questions

1. What does "worship" mean to you?
2. If praise is how we express joy, what are the things in your life that you spend the most time praising and telling people about, and why?
3. When is it most difficult for you to praise God?
4. What "trains of thought" are the hardest for you to stop?
5. What truths about God might help you stop your trains?

eleven

People

Why Loving Others Unleashes Us

Loving someone liberates the lover as well as the beloved.[1]

—Maya Angelou

On a cold November day in 1895, a boy named William was born. According to multiple sources who confirm this really did happen, his mother gave birth behind a bar, in Vermont, during a snowstorm. Somehow, both mother and child survived unharmed, and the following decade of William's life was rather ordinary.

At the age of eleven, William—Bill, as he came to be known—had his entire world shattered when his parents divorced, both choosing to leave him and his sister behind.[2] Bill's grandparents stepped in to raise the children, and for a time Bill seemed unfazed by the loss. By all appearances, he had weathered this second storm as well as he had the first. During his successful high school years he became captain of the football team, played violin for the orchestra, and was elected senior class president. He was resilient and seemingly unscathed by the wounds of his past. In reality, the pain was a bit like a splinter, buried deep in the skin and slowly working its way out.

About a year after high school, Bill met a woman by the name of Lois, a Brooklyn native who was four years his senior. In 1918 the two got married, just before he left to serve in World War I. Bill's time in the military was mostly unremarkable, but it was during those years that he made a decision that would alter the entire course of his life. One night at a dinner party, he decided to have a drink.[3]

Bill's grandfather was an alcoholic, making Bill an heir to an addictive disposition. His family history had remained latent until that night, but his first taste awakened a sleeping monster within. Bill quickly drank himself into a stupor, and it wasn't long before he was drinking heavily all the time.

When Bill returned home from the military, he enrolled in law school to make something of himself, but the addiction had already taken hold. Bill drank his way through law school, was too drunk to take his final exams, and never completed his degree.[4] Bill's drinking continued on this course for sixteen years, and at times he became so desperate he stole money from his wife and bankrupted her family.[5]

Bill wanted to stop drinking but he didn't know how, so in 1934, his wife took action. She checked him into a hospital for treatment, and Bill spent the following year getting sober, relapsing, and returning to the hospital several times.

It was during one of those hospital stays that an old drinking buddy paid Bill a visit. His friend had struggled with alcoholism too, but had found a way to get sober. The secret, he confided, was simple and modest: "Admit you are licked, get honest, talk it out, make restitution, give of yourself, and pray."[6] This advice, it would turn out, was the beginning of a whole new chapter in Bill's life.

Through treatment and coming to Christ, Bill quit drinking. His efforts to remain sober, and his desire to help others, gave birth to a support group, which we now know as Alcoholics Anonymous. Bill Wilson—or "Bill W." as he is remembered today—cofounded the organization to help individuals trapped by alcoholism. Today there are over 60,000 chapters in the United States, with over a million members.[7]

Alcoholics Anonymous (AA) is probably best known for its Twelve Step program, but it offers much more than a process. One of the most important functions of the group is the community it provides. Individuals can attend meetings for support, and members are paired with a "sponsor"—a sober, recovering alcoholic—who helps them along the way. Community is a linchpin of AA, not only because of the accountability it provides, but because of the mission it enlists people into. This latter role of community was an important part of Bill's own sobriety, which one biographer described this way: "While [Bill's] conversion experience was real, it was not what had kept him sober. He had been able to stay away from alcohol because of his efforts to help other alcoholics."[8] In other words, helping others helped him.

A friend of mine attends Alcoholics Anonymous, and I asked him about his own experience with AA's community. Had it helped him the way it helped Bill? He said that it had, and recalled a period of his own sobriety when he needed the "help of helping others": "What pulled me through this period was God's power and grace enabling me to get out of myself and help others. I'd leave the house with my 'problems' on the way to meet a new guy, and I'd drive home unable to recall those same problems just a couple of hours later."

This concept, that helping others helps you, was Bill's saving grace, and it continues to help people today. But Alcoholics

Anonymous is not unique in this sense. Countless organizations have been similarly inspired, as if the natural outworking of pain is to help others. Breast cancer survivors raise millions of dollars for research. Parents of children with disabilities become fierce advocates. Victims of abuse raise awareness for other victims. Each of these movements demonstrates the powerful truth that when you turn your pain into love for others, it helps you.

At the heart of that redemptive impulse is something deep and true, rooted in the creation of the universe. We see it most clearly in times of trial and suffering, when it leaps forth like a survival mechanism, and it reveals something basic to our design. In those moments of crisis, we discover that an essential path to human healing and wholeness is to love people.

God's Plan for Your Pain (*All* of It)

Whether or not you grew up in the church, you have probably heard of the Ten Commandments. The Old Testament book of Exodus tells us that the Ten Commandments were given to Moses directly from God. They include prohibitions against stealing, murdering, and committing adultery, and many modern societies are based upon these codes. Most people know this about the Ten Commandments, but what a lot of people *don't* know is that the commandments are about much more than law and order. They also tell us about the heart of God.

No one has revealed this heart better than Jesus, who came to "fulfill" the law (Matt. 5:17) and was the "culmination" of the law (Rom. 10:4). Throughout his life, Jesus showed us God's intention for the law, but in Matthew 22 he spelled it out plainly. Jesus boiled down all the commandments to two simple instructions:

> *"Love the Lord your God with all your heart and with all your soul and with all your mind." This is the first and greatest commandment.*

And the second is like it: "Love your neighbor as yourself." (vv. 37–39, emphasis mine)

Love God. Love others. According to Romans 13:9, the whole law can be "summed up" in those four words, and for most of my life I have tried to live by them. But here's what I always got wrong: for too long, I viewed these commands as "good Christian behavior." Much like reading the Bible, I filed these under the "shoulds" of following Jesus. *Of course* God wants us to love others. That's the nice thing to do.

What I'm discovering, however, is that God's desire has always been much bigger and better than being good. God doesn't ask us to love others simply because it's the right thing to do. God asks us to love others because it glorifies him and it heals something deep inside of us. In the same way that loving and praising God is a path to joy, there is a second way to joy, which is loving people. If you can get to that place of turning your pain into love, God will pull you out of yourself and heal you in a way that self-care cannot.

Put another way, the bend of redemption is outward. Our struggles drive us toward dependence on God and connection with others. When we turn our gaze outward, rather than crumpling inward, our souls take their first steps toward wholeness.

But here's the catch: many times, we limit this redemptive work to our biggest wounds, while ignoring or brushing off the smaller ones. Tragedy, grief, and loss have a way of naturally turning us outward, because they lay us flat on our backs. We can't ignore the pain because it's too consuming. In those moments, when we don't know how we're going to survive, we gasp for redemption like we would for air in our lungs.

However, we are less likely to look for redemption in the small stuff, like feeling unattractive or unprepared. Our small cuts seem too trivial. In those moments, when we feel a flush of embarrassment or a tinge of failure, we don't typically think, "How can God use this for good?" Instead, we either try to move on quickly, or we wallow in hurt feelings and self-doubt.

For most of my life, that's how I handled the small stuff. I balled up my fists and tried to get over it, or I pitied myself and shrank back. I never saw insecurity as an opportunity to love people better. I rarely turned my thoughts any higher than myself, so I remained stuck in my own self-focus. In doing so, I failed to recognize that no wound, and no experience of insecurity, is below the redemptive work of God. No matter how little or inconsequential the bruise, God can use it for more. When we assume our wounds are below the attention of God, we choose not to invite him into them. We stop redemption at the door.

Turning Insecurity into Love

To put some handles on this principle, I want to share two stories of what this outward-facing, people-loving redemption looks like in my life.

The first began with a conversation in Texas. It was wintertime in Austin, and I sat curled in an armchair at a trendy hotel. I was there to chat with a woman I was just beginning to know, and we happened to be in town at the same time. She was a few stages ahead of me in life, a great listener, and a wise woman of God. Because of these qualities and more, I had turned to her for counsel.

We were seated opposite one another as I described the agony of my smallness. I was ashamed of how insecure I was acting, but I had no other outlet for my emotions. I vented my heart in a loopy tangle of thoughts, and she nodded sympathetically at my aching.

At the close of my verbal dump, I turned to her and asked what she thought. How did she handle exclusion? What had she learned in her own experience?

Her answer was the beginning of a huge shift in my thinking. At the time, she was the women's ministry director at a megachurch out West. Her ministry was large and easy to get lost in, so whenever she experienced her own feelings of rejection or loneliness, she embraced them for their insight. The way she saw it, her feelings were a window into the experience of others. She explained, "A lot of women walk through the doors of my ministry, and they feel alone. They feel small, overwhelmed, or overlooked. Whenever I have those feelings myself, it helps me to remember those women. It helps me understand how they feel, and that helps me to care for them."

Her words flicked on a light in my brain. Rather than wiggle out from under my insecurity or shoo it away with affirmation, I could view my insecurities as a bridge. In fact, my insecurities could connect me to other women by helping me understand them in a way I hadn't before. I could receive my insecurities as preparation. My pain was foreshadowing future work, or as Rick Warren once described it, "God intentionally allows you to go through painful experiences to equip you for ministry to others."[9]

I began to see rejection in a different light. I asked God to write the pain onto my heart, not in the form of an open wound, but in the form of empathy. The world is full of lonely souls, and I never wanted to be too busy, too inconvenienced, too self-focused, or too bitter to stop and be Christ to them. I wanted my pain to give birth to mission, and that perspective became another ladder out of the pit.

The second story came several years later, through similar counsel from my longtime friend Renee. On this occasion, we met in a coffee shop in Charlotte, where we caught up on all things writing and life. She has been a writer for decades, so I was eager to pick her brain. I wanted to know how she maintained her focus on Jesus, and how she resisted the urge to compete.

Renee told me that one of her biggest temptations is the need to feel seen. She craves it, and it's easy to let that craving shape the way she does ministry. She discovered that the only way to release the grip of needing to be seen is to *see others*. That is to say, she goes out of her way to make others feel seen. If she's at a book signing, she makes time for every person. She looks women in the eyes. She listens to their stories. She hugs them. She is generous with her attention. By focusing on seeing others, she starves her own self-focus.

This made so much sense to me. When it comes to being seen, there is no end to the list of people whose attention you must win. There will always be someone else, someone impressive or important who you are desperate to feel noticed by. But if you can shift your focus off of yourself and onto others, it will set you free. Your love for others will become your healing.

Both of those conversations have changed the way I see insecurity, especially as it relates to others. Those two women helped me realize that the command to love others isn't just good, it's our joy. When insecurity strikes, the question we must ask ourselves is, *How can I turn this into love?* This question opens our eyes to the people we might have previously overlooked, and it prepares our hearts to care for them. Whether it's a crushing grief or a slight pang of insecurity, this question pulls us out of our soul-killing self-focus, and it shows us the way to resurrection, no matter the size of the death.

The Bigger Picture

I want you to pause and think for a moment. Do you know this ache? When insecurity or comparison or envy strikes your heart, do you feel it? Like actually *feel* it? Deep in your soul, do you notice how heavy it is?

I have felt it many times. Insecurity hurts. Making things about you that are not about you—it aches. And Jesus knew this, which is why he commanded us to love God and love others. He was putting his finger on a real wound, as if to say, "The weight of self-focus was never meant to be." It was never God's desire for us. We were never meant to treat everything in our lives like a measuring stick pointing back to us. We were never meant to carry that burden. That's why God doesn't simply *invite* us to throw the burden down; he *commands* it. In essence, he commands us to be free.

I love that about God and his Word. God wrote freedom into the heart of his law. It's a truth we often miss, because we assume the law is about rules or about being good, but that was never the point. God knows better than anyone else that there is something small and deeply unsatisfying about living a life for yourself. So he graciously calls us out of it, and into much more.

All of that is true and good and a reason to rejoice, but we can't stop there. The problem with self-focus is not simply what it does to our souls, but what it does to the world. When we are so distracted with ourselves and our own lives, we never get to the work of actually living out our faith. There is a whole world out there of brokenness and poverty and hunger and pain, begging to hear the good news of Christ, but we will never reach them if we're too focused on building our best lives now. That is Satan's great achievement: using good, true messages of Jesus to steal our attention from Jesus's work.

That is something we cannot stand for. Any teaching that promises peace without calling us out into the world to go bring peace is not the message of the gospel. Following Jesus means just that—*following him*—and we can't do that if our eyes are on ourselves instead of the cross.

Friends, the world desperately needs people who love well. This broken world is crying out for people who will love with the same abandon as Christ. And that kind of love will not spring forth from a people focused on themselves. When our focus is on our own needs, our own preferences, and our own comforts, we will not love people in a way that resembles anything like the love of Jesus.

Yes, loving people is a key to abundant life. Yes, God designed a world in which you love yourself *by* loving others. Yes, when you give you will receive. But none of these truths spins on the axis of self. It is not about you, and it *cannot* be about you, if you want to live the life God created you to live.

Focus Verse

"Dear friends, since God so loved us, we also ought to love one another. No one has ever seen God; but if we love one another, God lives in us and his love is made complete in us."—1 John 4:11–12

Focus Prayer

Lord Jesus, you have loved me so extravagantly. Thank you for coming near, and for laying down your life, so that I might have life too. Your love casts out fear and death, and I want to embody that same kind of love. When I love people with Christlike love, it will cast out fear and death in myself and in the people around me. I want to witness to the power of your love, so help me love people the same radical way you do. Amen.

Discussion Questions

1. Can you remember a time when helping someone helped you?
2. What is the "small stuff" in your life that you tend to ignore, instead of handing it over to God so that he can redeem it?

3. How do your insecurities keep you from loving people well?

4. When you think about your biggest insecurities or fears, what would it look like to "turn those into love" for others?

5. As a result of your wounds and insecurities, who are the people God might be calling you to see and serve better?

twelve

Purpose
Why Your Freedom Has a Form

> One of the best ways to face this problem of self-centeredness
> is to discover some cause and some purpose, some loyalty
> outside of yourself and give yourself to that something.[1]
> —Martin Luther King Jr.

*L*ove God. Love people. That is the call on everyone who claims
the name of Christ. When we answer the call, Jesus works all
kinds of miracles inside us and out.

But there's more.

When we love God and love people in our *particularity*, with our
gifts and our interests, in the ways that are specific to us, something
electric happens: we experience a sense of purpose. Maybe you've
experienced this yourself—it's almost visceral. When you find and
pursue your purpose, you can feel it in your bones. It's exhilarating

and motivating, even when it's hard. That's what is so powerful about purpose. It's not all hearts and rainbows. It doesn't always feel good, and it's certainly not easy, but it is compelling. For me in my life, nothing represents that strange mix of hard and good better than the birth of my son.

When I was nine months pregnant with our first child, my husband and I attended the mandatory hospital tour. I don't remember much about where we went or what we learned, but I will never forget previewing the delivery room. There was a couch, a chair, a pastel watercolor hanging on the wall, and at the center of it all was a bed with retractable stirrups. Our tour guide described a "normal" birth scenario while I stood there frozen like a tree. I had boarded a train with only one destination, and there I was, looking right at it.

I stared at the table and tried to imagine myself pushing out a baby. I glanced down at the planet protruding from my midsection and wondered, "Is this really going to work?" The logistics were not adding up. How could a baby come out *that way*? It just didn't make any sense. But sure enough, several weeks later, I was in a room identical to that one, ready to meet my son. Twenty-four hours into labor, I had developed preeclampsia and had endured a dose of magnesium, but it was finally time to push. I expected the delivery to be just as grueling as the labor, but it only lasted fifteen minutes. Three solid pushes later, Isaac came tumbling into the world.

The answer was yes. It did "work."

In the weeks following my son's birth, I recounted the delivery story again and again, and I marveled at what my body had done. In spite of my doubts, it had happened just like it was supposed to. For months, I couldn't get over that fact, and I remember how empowered I felt. "My body did what it was designed to do!" I gushed to a friend. "For the first time in my life, I feel like my body did what God created it to do."

That empowerment and sense of purpose is why many women "forget" the pain of childbirth. Labor can be long and hard and scary, but many mothers describe a unique sense of purpose through it, which makes them feel strong and alive. Of course, every birth story is different, and not every experience is the same, but for me, labor and delivery birthed a fresh sense of purpose. Mere weeks after I had delivered Isaac, I wanted to do it again, and that is the power of purpose. It awakens something inside of us so that we feel fully alive.

In this chapter, I want to focus on the power of purpose, and in particular the power of *your* purpose, the purpose that no one else has. Your purpose is the place where loving God and loving others meets your particularity. It also goes by the name of "calling," and it's one of the most delightful ways God draws us out of ourselves and into him.

Finding Your Purpose

When I was in school earning my doctoral degree, I got to do something amazing. As part of my research, I sat down with women enrolled in three evangelical seminaries across the country, and I asked them to tell me their stories. I asked them why they felt called to ministry and who encouraged them. I asked why they decided to attend seminary when so few of their peers do the same. I asked them about their vision for the church, their passion for the world, and their dreams for the future. After nearly every conversation, I walked away inspired. God is raising up a formidable force of women. Their gifts were as clear as day, and it was a thrill to glimpse their journeys up close. It was like getting a sneak peek of the story God is writing.

One of the themes that emerged from those conversations was the power of calling. When a woman felt called to ministry, that calling was more influential than just about any other factor in her life. This finding surprised me, because I would have predicted some other influential factor, like personality. I expected the women to be self-assured, outgoing, natural leaders who were fueled by godly ambition. And some of them were. But not all of them. Many, if not most, had been plagued by self-doubt. Some of the women even fled God's calling. I heard "Jonah stories" of women who avoided God's call until they couldn't resist it any longer. I heard "Abraham stories" of women who "obeyed and went," even though they didn't know where they were going (Heb. 11:8). As for doubts, they ranged all over. Some women worried their education was impractical or selfish. Why spend the money if they might not get a job? One woman worked for a parachurch ministry, and she feared her financial supporters would think it a waste. Other women were simply confused. They possessed pastoral gifts but they didn't feel called to be pastors, so they struggled to reconcile the two.

The sum of these conversations taught me a few things, and the first is that no calling is the same. This lesson is easy to detect in Scripture, in which Moses had a burning bush, Mary had an angel, Joseph had a dream, and Jonah had a fish. God can and does use anything to call his people, which means that no matter the call—whether it is to ministry or motherhood—we don't have to fit into a mold.

The second thing I learned is that God's calling is compelling. By worldly standards, it didn't make sense for those women to attend seminary. Both financially and practically, there were a lot of risks. There were many reasons to say no, which is why so many of them did for a while. And yet, something inside them couldn't resist forever. Something inside them knew they were disobeying God. I suspect they also knew, deep down, that God had created them for more. Their lives were chock full of signposts—their gifts, their interests, the affirming words of their parents, pastors, and friends—all pointing to their created purpose. And so, over time, they yielded to God's beckoning.

The final lesson I learned is that God's calling is fulfilling. One of the striking consistencies of these stories was a clear "before and after." Before these women said yes to God, they were plagued by doubt and unease. Instead of peace they felt confusion and fear. However, as soon as they took the plunge, everything changed. The internal struggle subsided, the doubts abated, and their minds were no longer filled with "what ifs." Did they still have doubts? Of course. Did they still have fears? You bet. But the peace that "transcends all understanding" (Phil. 4:7) had settled over their shoulders like a warm blanket. And for most of them, they never looked back.

The Power of Purpose

As I listened to each one of their stories, I detected echoes of my own. Throughout my life I faced my own leaps of faith, and each involved a lot of fear and trembling. I prayed and fasted and begged for clarity. Sometimes I truly wrestled with God. There was the time I turned down a job opportunity, and the time I walked away from a seminary I had dreamed of attending, all because I sensed the Spirit's "no." Each time, I doubted. "Surely this isn't what you have for me," I argued. "It doesn't make any sense!" Then, after summoning the courage to jump in faith, I discovered peace was already there waiting for me.

Like the women I interviewed, I also related to the deep fulfillment of using my gifts. I am a mother of two small boys, so it's easy to fill my time with them. There is always more cleaning, more laundry, more cuddling, which I could do all day every day. Except for one thing: it's not my only calling. As I go about my days tending my home, I hear the Spirit inviting me to meet him at my desk. When I write, I connect with God in a way that I don't anywhere else, and nothing restores me like using my talents for God.

And this all gets tricky. My kids are young and needy, which means sometimes my callings conflict. When they do compete, writing is the first to get crowded out, and when that happens, I slowly start to wither. I become short-tempered and restless, feeling a bit like a clogged spring, the pressure building until it explodes. Without a healthy vent for my passions and my gifts, I turn into an emotional geyser, erupting at unpredictable times.

When my husband and I notice this happening, we adjust. We get creative and find time for me to write. It takes some flexibility on his part, so I initially felt selfish about it. It seems like such a luxury to accommodate me, and to some extent, it is. Not every season or financial situation affords that kind of margin. In that sense, it is a luxury. But selfish? No. Our gifts are meant to be used. God grants us our abilities, not to set them on a shelf but to build up his church. As long as our motives are for God's glory, our work is not selfish but ordained. Once I was able to embrace that truth, I experienced abundance in both my callings. The time I took to write made me a better wife, mom, and follower of Christ.

My story, and the stories of the women in seminary, all point to the power of purpose, but the very best story comes straight out of God's Word. Remember Paul in Philippians? Remember his joy in suffering? Paul, in his bleakest hour, was still able to declare, "I have learned the secret of being **content in any and every situation**, whether well fed or hungry, whether living in plenty or in want" (4:12, emphasis mine). Paul's example is extraordinary, and we have already discussed the secret of his joy, which was his singular focus on Christ. However, this contentment will still escape us if we imagine Paul sitting on the floor having warm and fuzzy thoughts about Jesus. Contentment was not a passive experience for Paul. The other half of Paul's secret was his purpose.

You see, Paul wasn't sitting in prison twiddling his thumbs. Even in chains, he was a man on a mission. In Philippians 1:13 he shares, "It has become clear throughout the whole palace guard and to everyone else that I am in chains for Christ." In other words, Paul was strategic with his state. While under arrest, Paul was likely under twenty-four-hour surveillance, which meant he was chained to his guards. They watched over him in shifts, and Paul seized on his circumstances as an opportunity. Paul's captors were a captive audience, so he shared the gospel with them. As a result, the entire palace guard learned about Christ.

That was the secret of Paul's contentment. He didn't simply will himself to feel content. Instead, he looked for the purpose in his imprisonment. He figured out how to love God and love others in his particular situation, and that sense of purpose was a part of his joy.

In her now viral TED Talk, psychologist Kelly McGonigal had this to say about purpose: "Chasing meaning is better for your life than avoiding discomfort."[2] It's counterintuitive, but this explains the illogical joy of purpose. It's the reason women go to seminary when the risks are high and the obstacles tall. It's the reason women "forget" the pain of childbirth and crave the experience again. It's the reason my husband and I make sacrifices so that I can continue to write. And it's how Paul found contentment despite the difficulty of his circumstances. Each story points to the defiant power of purpose, and the common thread running throughout each one is an outward-facing focus. Each story is driven by a love for God and others. When we embrace our God-given purpose, he draws our focus off of ourselves and onto a much bigger story.

Selfless Ambition

I wonder if you noticed something. In the stories about women in seminary, and the story of my own negotiation with calling, a common word showed up: *selfish*. When you step into your purpose, it is so fulfilling and gratifying that, for some of us, it sends up a red flag. Especially for those of us who grew up expecting our lives to involve loads of sacrifice and suffering. In her book *Teach Us to Want*, Jen Pollock Michel shares her own wrestling with this question: "Is it true that the hardest, least desirable choice is the most obviously holy? Is it true that personal desire must never be trusted? Am I right to immediately incriminate ambition?" She adds, "Many, like me, imagine desire and faith in a boxing ring, facing off like opponents."[3]

Like Michel, I sometimes wonder if God would possibly call me to something I love. The voice of this worry grows louder when my calling doesn't make sense. When you have to slice the household income in order to stay home with the kids, or take a financial risk by going back to school, it can feel selfish. When a calling we love requires sacrifice—particularly sacrifice from others—we can't help but wonder if our motivations are wrong.

So, how do we resolve this?

Michel's advice initially surprised me. She neither condemns our selfish ambitions nor commissions us to "follow our dreams." Instead she picks a third way: be honest about your sin. In both godly callings and self-centered ones, sin inevitably creeps in. It's the nature of being human, which means selfish motives tell us little about whether or not we are actually called. In our brokenness, we can take the best and noblest callings and twist them toward self-centered ends, so it's good to be clear-eyed about that. The corruption of a godly plan says nothing about the plan and everything about us, so we shouldn't throw the baby out with the bathwater. That's why Michel concludes, "Growing into maturity doesn't mean abandoning our desires, but growing in our discernment of them."[4] We don't have to be afraid of our selfish desires, but we do need to admit them. When we do, we open the door to God's grace in our lives, so that he can identify the good and prune our hearts of the bad. Dave Harvey once wrote, "A good ambition becomes a selfish ambition when it's our only ambition."[5] Our calling isn't the problem so much as the way we prioritize it.

The way we navigate the work of discernment is a careful process of discovering our gifts, seeking the Holy Spirit, and receiving feedback from our community. So talk to your family. Talk to your friends. Ask your pastors. What do they say? What do they see in you? I always encourage people to survey their friends, because you might be surprised by what they tell you. Community helps us to see things in us that we cannot see ourselves.

Another reason to discern our God-given purpose is that it actually saves us from selfish ambition. Without a godly purpose guiding our lives, we inevitably settle for something less. We were, after all, created for purpose, so our souls strain after it. We are always on a search for purpose and meaning, whether we recognize the urge or not. Even if we haven't identified a calling, we gravitate toward purpose like a second home. Whether it's advancing at work, starting a hobby, or leading a book club, we all look for places where our interests and ambitions give us meaning.

In the absence of true purpose, we fall into lesser purposes. There are the nosy neighborhood busybodies, the gossips spreading rumors under the guise of concern, the internet ranters who are zealous to speak the "truth," or the codependent romances of people who need to be needed. There are a million different ways we seek meaning and significance, but they cannot fulfill us the way our created purpose can. In his book *Rising to the Call*, Os Guinness describes the emptiness of these lesser pursuits:

> All other standards of success—wealth, power, position, knowledge, friendship—grow tinny and hollow if we do not satisfy this deeper longing. For some people, the hollowness leads to what Henry David Thoreau described as "lives of quiet desperation"; for others, the emptiness and aimlessness deepen into a stronger despair.[6]

That hollowness and despair is why Scripture is so stern about idleness. Ecclesiastes 4:5 warns, "Fools fold their hands and ruin themselves," while 1 Timothy 5 instructs young widows not to "get into the habit of being idle and going about from house to house. And not only do they become idlers, but also busybodies who talk nonsense, saying things they ought not to" (v. 13). In the vacuum of purposelessness, our inward-bending souls turn toward empty pursuits.

How do we discern the difference between God-given purposes and lesser ones? Just look at their fruits. A God-given purpose, hemmed in by the boundaries of Sabbath, Spirit, Scripture, and wise counsel, will produce love, joy, peace, patience, kindness, goodness, faithfulness, gentleness, and self-control (Gal. 5:22–23). Lesser purposes manifest in behavior like gossip, busybodying, stressing, and raging. They parade all over the internet as scrutiny, name-calling, and endless empty hours on Pinterest. In the absence of true purpose, we swing between outrage and insecurity, judging other parents on their parenting or tearing down strangers out of envy. We do this because we're desperate for validation and meaning. What appears to be pettiness or self-righteousness is often a soul crying out for significance.

That's why I spent my entire doctoral degree trying to understand calling and purpose, and why I am so passionate about people using their gifts. It *matters*. It matters to God, and it matters to every single person around you. The body of Christ is interdependent, and each one of us plays a necessary part. Best of all, this purpose is for our good. When we identify our purpose and use our gifts for God, it's fulfilling. It makes us more like Christ, it delivers us from worthless endeavors, and it saves us from the quiet desperation of living for ourselves.

Focus Verse

"Each of you should use whatever gift you have received to serve others, as faithful stewards of God's grace in its various forms." —1 Peter 4:10

Focus Prayer

Lord, I know you created me for a purpose. Help me to know what that purpose is. Send people who can name my calling and cultivate my talents, so that I can use them for your glory. Guide me along the path you marked out for me, so that I can experience the joy and fullness of my unique creation and honor you above all. Amen.

Discussion Questions

1. What experiences have given you the greatest sense of purpose?
2. What obstacles did you face, and how did your sense of purpose help you through them?
3. When you read the statement, "Chasing meaning is better for your life than avoiding discomfort," did that resonate with you? Why or why not?
4. Have you ever wrestled with feeling selfish about your calling? And if so, what was the source of your guilt?
5. What are some practical ways to sort out your healthy motives from your selfish ones?

Thirteen

Passion

Why the Humble Are So Free

We must die if we are to live. There is no spiritual life for
you, for me, for any man, except by dying into it.[1]

—Charles Spurgeon

am a Passion kid.

In case you don't know what I'm referring to, the Passion conferences were launched in the late 1990s by Louie
and Shelley Giglio, with the aim of reaching young people ages
eighteen to twenty-five. I attended my first event in the early 2000s,
and for years after, I joined tens of thousands of college students
each year in heart-thumping, delirious praise. Those conferences
were a big part of my spiritual growth, and over a decade later I
can still recall key moments from those days. I remember listening

to the likes of Francis Chan and Beth Moore, who preached inspiring messages about living for Jesus. I remember John Piper delivering a withering rant against retirement. "I'll tell you what a tragedy is!" he shouted, before skewering the American dream of retiring at the beach. "You will come to the end of your life," he thundered, "and the last great work you give account to your Creator will be 'Here it is, Lord. My *shell collection*.' THAT is a tragedy."[2]

As a nineteen-year-old, I ate it up with a spoon. "I WILL NEVER RETIRE!" I vowed. I was all-in. I was ready to live passionately for Jesus.

A couple years ago, I returned to Passion with our church's college students. Walking into that arena was like stepping into a time machine. It took me back to the days when I was idealistic and uncompromising, ready to take on the world. I was filled with nostalgia as I scanned the foggy, neon-lit space, the thousands of hands raised in worship. I peered at the young faces around me, and I couldn't help but wonder,

What would my twenty-two-year-old self think of me now? Would she be proud? Or disappointed?

My hunch is that it would be the latter. I'm not nearly as impressive as I thought I would be. My life is a lot quieter and more ordinary, and I haven't accomplished all that I dreamed. There are good reasons for that, and bad reasons too, but in that moment at the conference, I mostly felt grateful for the reminder. Back in those days, I was naïve as a newborn lamb, but I sure did run hard after God. Whatever parts of my desires were pure and Christ-centered, I want to keep pace with them today.

At the same time, my dreams back then were not entirely Christ-centered. They were a whole lot of self-centered too. When I listened to the speakers, wide-eyed and in awe, the truth is I wanted to be them. I thought "passion" meant energy and emotion and LOUD, and that leadership meant preaching to masses. Passion, for me, was thoroughly entangled with my own broken craving for glory.

What God has taught me in the fifteen years since is that true passion is something else entirely. Rarely is it glamorous—it has more to do with sacrifice than strong emotion. The word itself comes from the Latin root *passio*, which means "suffering" or "enduring." This definition is the reason Christians have, for centuries, called Jesus's death "the Passion of Christ."

In that sense, "passion" is a willingness to join Christ in his suffering, and as a young twentysomething, I was not ready for that. I thought I was, and I would have said I was, but the reality is I had no idea. It's easy to commit yourself to suffering and dying for Jesus when you suspect it will never be required of you.

What I didn't realize back then—and if I'm being honest, what I am still trying to wrap my mind around today—is that "laying yourself down" is not optional. It's not the bad luck of persecuted Christians in far-off lands. It's not for some Christians but not others. Laying yourself down *is* the call. We cannot escape it. Whether we live on a mission field in a hostile land or in a wholesome neighborhood in our own hometown, we are guaranteed hardship and humiliation because we live in a broken world. Our physical lives might never be required of us, but resurrection was never about just our physical bodies. Everything, every nook and cranny of our beings, must be entirely reborn, which also means everything must die.

In the course of the Christian life, God sets about the careful work of putting to death everything inside of us that needs to die. Every idol, every fear, every lie, every reflex that rebels against his goodness and love. He puts it all to death, and a lot of times it hurts. A lot. It feels like an actual death. But it's the one and only way to resurrection and life. That's why another important practice for forgetting yourself is *passion*, or dying to self.

Dying to Live

The story of my insecurity—the loneliness, the pain of feeling small, the needing to be seen and praised—all of it was the story of God putting things to death in me. He was killing things inside me because they were killing me, though I didn't realize it at the time. I don't think many of us do. We get so focused on the pain and figuring out how to escape it that we cannot recognize God's intentions.

That was my story. For years, I missed it. I thought insecurity and loneliness were trials God was delivering me from, not through. I also failed to recognize the tool for this painful work, which was school. I spent four and a half years completing my PhD, and during that time I struggled. The source of it all was not the classwork itself, but rather the timing of it. The year before I enrolled at Trinity Evangelical Divinity School, I had sensed God calling me to write full-time. The dream of writing had been in my heart for years, and I had finally decided to pursue it. After prayer and seeking counsel, I left my job and I gave my whole focus to this call.

Six months later, God added a twist. He opened the door for me to return to school. It fell into place in a way that was clearly from God, but I was also very confused. I thought writing was the plan, not school, and the timing didn't make sense at all. How could I possibly do both?

When I first started my classes I had some extra margin to write, but that balance was only temporary. Two years into my degree, we had our first son. Two years later, I got pregnant again. Throughout it all, I kept writing, but it was getting harder. I declined writing opportunities I would have liked to take, and my dreams moved further away. I loved being in school and I loved being a mom, but I burned with envy at my writing friends. I watched as each one published her first book, then her second, while I spent my time combing through academic journals.

During that season, I felt a bit like Joseph, a man with a dream deferred. He was given a call and then thrown in a pit, and I could relate to his heartache. Only instead of a pit, I was in a library basement.

Whether or not you're a writer, you may have had a similar experience. Maybe you put your career on hold to become a stay-at-home mom, maybe you can't afford to go back to school, or maybe you keep getting passed over for a leadership position at church. Whatever the situation, many of us experience a disconnect between calling and opportunity. We know we heard God's voice, but nothing happened afterward. Or worse, the barriers grew taller. In that place between calling and opportunity, it can feel like our gifts have been buried. And that's how I felt. I thought my gifts were going to waste, so I became impatient and discontent.

In reality, God never wastes our gifts (Matt. 25:14-30; Luke 11:33). God gives us gifts because he intends to use them, but the process is rarely a straight line. If he had plucked me out of that Passion conference and placed me in the fullness of my call, I would have self-destructed. I was too self-focused, too full of pride, too motivated by my own need for glory. There were unhealthy things in my heart that needed to die, and that's what God was doing in the "pit."

What I eventually learned through that season is that my gifts hadn't been buried. They had been planted. In John 12:24, Jesus says, "Unless a kernel of wheat falls to the ground and dies, it remains only a single seed. But if it dies, it produces many seeds." God doesn't bury our gifts, but he does sow them. He plants them in fertile ground where they can grow deep and sturdy roots. He sows them in the depths of the soil where they are safe from the scorching light of attention or the choking thorns of pride. God plants our gifts so that one day they can flourish, but the planting can feel like a burial. It's dark. The work in the ground is hidden. When God plants our gifts, it can feel like a death.

My time in school was a time in the soil. God had planted my gifts, and it felt like a death, but it was only a death like a kernel. He wasn't really burying me but preparing me to live, which meant I had to die to myself.

Now, I would love to tell you I received it all with grace, that I was noble and poised and brave. But I wasn't. Many days, I was a mess. I doubted myself and I doubted God's plans. I tried to avoid the pain, or numb it with lots of positive self-talk. I sought temporary relief by comparing myself to people who made me feel like a success. I ran to all my old idols for help, and I fought against God as he wrestled them out of my fingers. I didn't want the life he was offering, because I wanted the life I wanted, and that was that.

I remained in that struggle for years. I wanted the resurrection without the death. I refused God's invitation to die to myself, while ignoring the parts of myself that were already dead.

If you recall the interview I mentioned earlier in the book, the one between Jennie Allen and Christine Caine, Caine shared one other nugget of wisdom that changed my perspective on the "pit" of school. She drew a comparison between leadership development and developing photographs. Photos, she explained, are developed in a darkroom, where the negatives are placed in harsh chemicals. The process is literally dark, and not a shred of light can break in, because exposure will ruin the photos. Leaders, she continued, are formed the same way. God brings us into the darkroom to develop the image of Christ in us, but most of us don't want to go in. So we opt out. We find shortcuts and we strain after the spotlight before our development is complete. All of this undermines God's perfect process:

> We don't allow the image of God to form in us, which is only ever formed through suffering, through trials, through being overlooked, through being talked about, through being hurt, through being

unapproved, through being unapplauded, when you're left out and everyone else is included, when people are being celebrated and you are not, when you're not invited to the table. Those are the things that actually make you.[3]

Naming this truth was a breakthrough for me. I had never viewed my insecurities and loneliness as a darkroom of spiritual development. Instead, I retreated from them and strained after the light. I found artificial ways to make myself big, to feel important, seen, and known. At the very same time that God was freeing me of self-focus, I turned to self-focus to save me.

Feeling Better versus Being Better

No one ever warned me that dying to self feels like an actual death. As God lovingly crucified my self-focus, it nearly tore me in two. There were nights when I buried my face in my husband's chest and begged him to tell me something true. I was sure that if he used just the right words, in just the right order, I would somehow feel better. But my husband never could find those words. Nothing he said ever quite worked.

Of course, that wasn't my husband's fault. It was God's mercy, because he had no interest in making me feel better. He wasn't interested in numbing the pain with encouraging words, even with words that were true. Instead, God was interested in *making me better*—making me entirely new—and that meant putting to death the things inside me that were making me sick. My heart was wrapped so tightly around my idols that God's attack on them felt like an attack on me. But it was a grace. God was saving me from myself.

We have talked a lot about the book of Philippians, and Paul's incredible, death-defying joy. However, the core and centerpiece of the letter is Jesus's life, suffering, and death. It's the paradigm for

Paul's mind-set and ministry. It's the reason Paul has freedom and joy. After gazing on the life and sacrifice of Christ, Paul embodies its counterintuitive message, that the only way up is down, the only way to increase is to decrease, and the only way to glory is humility. In Philippians 2:5–11, Paul renders it this way:

In your relationships with one another, have the same mindset as Christ Jesus:

> *Who, being in very nature God,*
> *did not consider equality with God something to be used*
> *to his own advantage;*
> *rather, he made himself nothing*
> *by taking the very nature of a servant,*
> *being made in human likeness.*
> *And being found in appearance as a man,*
> *he humbled himself by becoming obedient to death—*
> *even death on a cross!*

> *Therefore God exalted him to the highest place*
> *and gave him the name that is above every name,*
> *that at the name of Jesus every knee should bow,*
> *in heaven and on earth and under the earth,*
> *and every tongue acknowledge that Jesus Christ is Lord,*
> *to the glory of God the Father.*

This is the blueprint of the Christian life, but here's what I don't want you to miss: the death and resurrection we are called into is not just a single event. Once we trust in the power of Jesus's death and resurrection, we receive the promise of future resurrection, *but* resurrection is also here and now. Our entire lives become a cycle of death and rebirth, death and rebirth, death and rebirth. Death and resurrection is not one far-off experience awaiting us in eternity, but an entire way of life. We die and are reborn again and again throughout our entire lives. Resurrection is not an end point but a door.

That's why God isn't interested in making us feel better. He has no use for superficial clichés or cutesy statements that make us feel good in the moment. Not if they keep us from doing the hard work of dying so that we can truly live. He is equally uninterested in reinforcing self-deception by allowing us to deny our own sickness. God wants us to see the parts of ourselves that are broken, so that we welcome his healing instead of denying we need it.

In his book *How to Survive a Shipwreck*, author Jonathan Martin asks, "What if God doesn't choose to save us in spite of our failures, losses, and embarrassments, but precisely through them?"[4] In other words, insecurity is not always an obstacle to the path; sometimes it *is* the path. That's the trouble with some messages about escaping insecurity: they are well-intentioned but sometimes incomplete. These half-baked approaches are easy to spot, because they only identify the lies of insecurity and nothing more. They remind us of our goodness, our "enough-ness," our belonging, and that is where they end.

However, if we really want to be delivered from insecurity, we can't stop there. There is no deliverance and no resurrection until we can admit that our insecurities contain both lies *and* truths. Insecurities feed us lies about ourselves and our worth, but they also reveal truths about our idols, our misplaced focus, or our misplaced priorities. Insecurity is a sign of spiritual sickness, and until we can admit that and confess it, we will never address the source of the pain. Nice words about our belonging only hide it for a while.

I know this is hard. Especially if you're in the thick of it. When you are writhing under the thumb of insecurity or shame, the only thing you want is out. You want it to be over, and that's my instinct too, but I am learning to see it all differently. The pain of self-focus and insecurity is like a scalpel: in the hands of the wrong person, it only slashes and maims. But in the hands of a capable surgeon, it's a tool for healing. The cut still hurts, but it's for our good, and suffering is the scalpel of God. In the hands of the Great Physician,

God can use pain and insecurity for our benefit. He can use them to humble us, to teach us, to grow us. He shows us the idols we're hiding and wrests them from our tired hands.

That is the strange, surprising, upside-down good news of Jesus Christ. Whenever you feel like a failure or a hack, whenever you worry that you're not a good parent or spouse, whenever you fear you're not enough or that you can't keep up with it all, there is a sense in which God responds, "Yes, that's true." And this is, amazingly, good news. You can be a failure. You can be "not enough." And then you can stop trying to make yourself big enough or capable enough to carry the weight of the world, because God never designed you to do it. Your shoulders will never be broad enough, and your back never that strong. Once you realize that, once you run smack up against the wall of your own limitations, it's a mercy. That's when you finally taste the freedom of no longer striving, of no longer trying to be what only God can be.

When God invites you into the painful work of dying to self, don't wave it off as an attack. Don't skip your way out of it with happy self-talk. Bat down the lies and send the accuser on his way, but accept the rest as a gift. The gift of smallness, of humility, of dying to self—it comes in an ugly package, but the most beautiful treasure is inside.

Focus Verse

"Very truly I tell you, unless a kernel of wheat falls to the ground and dies, it remains only a single seed. But if it dies, it produces many seeds."—John 12:24

Focus Prayer

Lord Jesus, you are the God of death and resurrection. Because of you, I can have life after death, but I cannot have life without death. Give me the courage to embrace your redemption, even when it hurts, and even when it feels like a death. I invite you to kill the things inside of me that are killing me. Prune the idols, prune the sin, prune the selfishness and self-doubt. Take it all, even if it hurts, because I don't have to fear humility or lowliness anymore. In the kingdom of God, the lowly are first and the humble are free. Thanks be to God.

Discussion Questions

1. After reading this chapter, what does the word "passion" mean to you?
2. When was a time when you felt like your gifts were invisible or buried?
3. Looking back, what do you think God was doing during that time?
4. This chapter talked about the "truths" revealed by our insecurities, truths about our idols and our fears. What truths do your insecurities reveal about you?
5. In what ways do you think God is asking you to die to yourself?

fourteen

Forgetting Yourself without Neglecting Yourself

His will for me points to one thing: the realization, the discovery, and the fulfillment of my self, my true self, in Christ.[1]

—Thomas Merton

One evening when my son was ten months old, I was giving him a bath before bed. Ike was out of town for his mom's retirement party, so it was just the two of us at home. My son splashed and squealed while I washed his soft skin, the suds streaming down his chest and his back. I cupped my hand over his eyes while I rinsed out his hair, and that was the moment I felt it. A strange pain in my stomach.

It began dull and short, so I ignored the discomfort. Probably indigestion, I thought. I dried Isaac off, slipped his pajamas over his head, and tried not to notice it growing. It started to come in waves of increasing intensity, so I put Isaac in his crib and balled up on the couch. If I laid still for a moment, I thought the pain might eventually pass. But it didn't. It only grew sharper.

It wasn't long before the pain became rhythmic, like the surges and rests of labor. I tried relaxing my body and taking deep breaths, while my mind screamed, "What is going on?" I called my husband and family but no one picked up, and I frantically considered my options. We were new to the area, but there was a woman from church who had recently given me her number. Minutes after I called and interrupted her dinner, she sprang through the front door and launched into action. She called an ambulance, found a sitter, and met me at the hospital, where we waited for the doctors to run tests. Not long after, we had our answer. The cause of it all was my gallbladder. I had what was called a "gallbladder attack."

I don't know about you, but prior to that day, "gallbladder attack" was not part of my vocabulary. I had never heard of such a thing—though I was about to learn a lot—and the first thing I learned was good news. With gallbladder attacks, the bark is worse than its bite. They're painful but they're generally not dire. The attack is triggered by gallstones that are, well, let's just say "moving," and that's why the pain comes in waves. The condition is not life-threatening but there is only one solution, which is that my gallbladder would have to come out.

Before that experience, I could count on one hand the number of times I had thought about my gallbladder. Or even *used* the word "gallbladder." (I promise I am almost done using the word "gallbladder.") I knew it was an organ somewhere inside my body, and that was pretty much it. I knew virtually nothing until it *attacked*, and then I became a gallbladder expert. That is the natural unfolding of things when you're dealing with an injury or illness. You take something for granted until it stops working, because ailments demand our attention.

The reason I share this story is that tucked into this pattern is a valuable spiritual principle. When a part of our selves is broken or wounded or sick, it consumes the bulk of our focus. Tim Keller describes the principle this way:

> Have you ever thought about the fact that you do not notice your body until there is something wrong with it? When we are walking around, we are not usually thinking how fantastic our toes are feeling. Or how brilliantly our elbows are working today. We would only think like that if there had previously been something wrong with them. That is because the parts of our body only draw attention to themselves if there is something wrong with them.[2]

That was my experience. My physical pain had turned my focus inward, and our souls do exactly the same. Self-focus, Keller explains, is a sign of something unwell. The self is "always drawing attention to itself" because it's sick and in need of healing. That's why the answer to self-focus is not just self-forgetfulness. If your self is wounded, then it needs mending.

To put it another way, if you come away from this book believing your personal health doesn't matter—whether it's emotional, spiritual, or physical—and that you simply need to focus on yourself less, I will have failed. The vision of this book is not possible without some essential healing inside you, and self-examination is a part of that process. Where we get ourselves in trouble is when our focus gets stuck and self-care evolves into self-focus. When that happens, self-focus *becomes* our sickness.

With that intention in mind, I want to look at two ways self-forgetfulness is confused with self-neglect, because self-forgetfulness never competes with our healing. It requires it. The first misapplication we're going to look at is "the martyr complex,"

179

and the second is a false belief that the "self" is bad. Both are distortions of the command to love God and others, so we will also look at some guardrails to keep us from veering off course.

The Martyr Complex

I sometimes tell people that "laziness" is my spiritual gift, and there is probably some truth to it. I am fiercely protective of my time and my energy. Saying no has never been a struggle for me. If I start to feel overwhelmed, I cut back on commitments like my hair is on fire. I rarely take on more than I can handle, because I hate feeling stressed out. I am also unafraid to ask for help.

I would love to say I do all this because I am wise and "honoring the Sabbath," but it's mostly that I like to have control. I like to play it safe. I don't like to walk by faith. I'm a "path of least resistance" kind of girl. Because of my predisposition toward ease, I run from the pressure to "do it all," and I buck the impossible expectations on women. I will never forget sitting at a women's church event while a speaker taught us how to plate our kids' food. She showed us a panda bear of beans and rice, and a ladybug made of sliced apples and raisins, and she was truly talented and creative. She was using her gifts to inspire other women, and for that, I should have celebrated her. Instead, I felt threatened. With all that I have going on, who has time to make a Mona Lisa out of ham? I turned to my table and whispered, "*You know you don't have to do that!*" as if I was saving them from something.

In hindsight, I wasn't helping those women at all, but imposing my own issues on them. Some women love those creative flourishes, while I saw them only as stress. Just "one more thing" I'd have to do. That's why my aversion to "doing it all" is both my downfall and my salvation. It saves me from a lot of unnecessary commitments, but it also makes me stingy and judgmental.

Now, I am well aware that not everyone possesses this "gift." For some of you, the pressure to do it all is *strong*. Maybe your kids are doing a million activities, or your work life is bleeding into your home life. Maybe you are leading too many committees because *someone* has to do it, or you struggle to say no even though you're already overextended. I think most of us recognize the soul-crushing power of "busy," but we still find ways to justify it. Maybe we "can't fall behind at work" or we want our kids "to have the same opportunities as everyone else," all of which seem legitimate. But too often what's really going on beneath these excuses is a mind-set called *the martyr complex*.

The martyr complex has the look of godliness, because its surface motivation is good. We want to take care of our family, or our friends, or our church, and the gospel does call us to hardship, doesn't it? If Jesus suffered, and I am suffering, then I must be on the right track. That is the logic of this mind-set. As a result, the martyr complex has driven many well-intentioned mothers to wring themselves dry. The image of the self-sacrificing, long-suffering parent hangs over us like a measuring stick from God. That's why the martyr complex seems selfless and loving, though it's more about guilt, shame, and pride. There can be love in there too, but the added motivations are what drive us to make unhealthy sacrifices.[3]

The martyr complex showed up in my own life when I began putting my oldest son in daycare. I was finishing my dissertation and pregnant with our second child, and I needed to finish school before he was born. I arranged for my son to go in two mornings a week, but I quickly realized it wasn't enough. I needed him to go three mornings instead, but I wouldn't admit it to myself. My son was only two years old, and three mornings seemed like too much. Plus, I wanted to be like those "other mothers" who "love being with their children all the time." (I have since learned these women do exist, but only in the way unicorns exist.) I felt guilty

181

for needing time away from my kid, so I decided to stick with our schedule, and my stress level quietly ballooned.

It didn't take long before Ike noticed my anxiety, so we put our heads together for a solution. We decided that "guilt" is not a motivation from God, and that our childcare provider was a blessing. She was, after all, a wise woman of God who knew more about children than we did. Her gifts were a reminder of why God gave us the church, so that we can raise our children *together*.

My story is similar to many women I know. Guilt, shame, and the pressure to keep up all lead us to make bad decisions. They leave us feeling worn out, run over, and agitated, all in the name of "sacrifice." Of course, sacrifice is sometimes required for our kids, but when is the sacrifice unhealthy? How are we to discern between Christlike sacrifice and the martyr complex?

Looking at my own life, I see two key filters to help us distinguish between them, and the first is **motives**. If our sacrifices are motivated by guilt, shame, or a need to keep up, then the sacrifices are probably not healthy. They are also, on some level, fundamentally about us, because we are primarily motivated by image. If any part of our motivation is rooted in comparison or the desire to be good enough, then the pressure is not from God.

In contrast with guilt-motivated forms of sacrifice, Jesus's sacrifice overcame guilt. Hebrews 12:2 says Jesus endured the cross while "scorning its shame," meaning his humiliation was a direct affront to shame. Don't miss the difference here: one sacrifice is *motivated by* shame, while the other *overcomes* shame. Shame and guilt are not God's tools for motivation, but his enemy's.

The second way we distinguish between Christlike sacrifice and the martyr complex is the **consequences** of our sacrifice. More specifically, what happens to your soul? How is your emotional and spiritual well-being? Are you stressed out or rested? Peaceful or anxious? Joyful or angry all the time?

In Acts 7:54–60, we read about the stoning of Stephen, a man "full of the Holy Spirit" (v. 55). As the stones pelted his body, he lovingly cried, "Lord, do not hold this sin against them" (v. 60). Stephen's words echo those of Jesus on the cross—"Father, forgive them, for they do not know what they are doing" (Luke 23:34)— and this similarity tells us something about sacrifice. The way we discern between godly sacrifice and self-motivated sacrifice is that one makes us more like Jesus. The martyr complex leaves a wake of frayed nerves, short tempers, and constant worry, while Christlike sacrifice has the look of our Savior. Like Stephen, like Paul, we exude joy, peace, and patience, even when it doesn't make sense.

Before moving on to the second distortion, I want to address a fear related to this one. One of the things that encourages the martyr complex is a belief (and an anxiety) that we follow a punishing God. We wonder if God will lead us down the hardest path possible for no other reason than to grow us. This mind-set sees God as a stern, glowering father, eager to discipline us with force. At the first sign of pride or independence, this strict God will correct us with pain.

If you can relate to this grim view of God, I want to remind you of two truths. The first is that God is our Father, and if you are a parent (or if you have friends who are), you know the tenderness of a parent's heart for their child. Parents do not delight to watch their kids suffer, and they will do anything to spare them the pain. Yes, parents enforce discipline and the discipline hurts, but it's only dispensed as a last resort. Our heavenly Father is the same. His desire is to shepherd us, not rake us over the coals. He never delights to undo us.

The second truth to assure us is the entire book of Proverbs, which is devoted to avoiding unnecessary suffering. Again and again, Proverbs contrasts the way of foolishness with the way of wisdom. It provides practical steps away from peril and toward the righteous life. The word *God* is only mentioned a handful of times, but the entire book is about his intentions. God doesn't sit in heaven scheming new ways to make us suffer. He is more interested in rescuing us from suffering.

The "Self" Is Bad

When I was single and in my twenties, I did what many singles in their twenties do, which was to make unwise romantic decisions. Each relationship was different, and each is its own story, but each one had a basic pattern. Because they were good men who seemed a great fit on paper, I casually ignored the Spirit's prompting. I bulldozed through wisdom and counsel from friends, because why wouldn't God want me to date a nice Christian man?

Of course, it all ended the way you would expect: at worst, I was devastated, and at best, I lost a friend. When I looked back on each relationship and wondered what went wrong, I couldn't deny my own blindness. Deep down, on some level, I knew I should have slowed down, or I should have said no altogether. But what I wanted more than to listen to God was to have a boyfriend.

Your romantic history might look different than mine, but folly is something we all know. A decision was wrong for us, perhaps blatantly wrong, but we decided to go for it anyway. Whether it's dating, visiting a certain website, or landing a well-timed jab, there is a spiritual tug-of-war inside us. We know the good and might even want to do it, but we fail again and again.

This tension is even present in our struggles with self-focus. No matter how much we want to focus on God, it doesn't just happen on its own. We know God is central, and we want to give him priority, but something keeps pulling us inward.

In Romans 7:15, Paul reveals a battle within himself, a breakdown between knowing what is godly and living it: "I do not understand what I do. For what I want to do I do not do, but what I hate I do." In Matthew 26, Jesus pinpoints the problem's source, warning, "The spirit is willing but the flesh is weak" (v. 41). Both Jesus and Paul blame the influence of the "flesh," a term Christians often misunderstand. Contrary to assumption, the "flesh" is not our physical bodies, nor does it refer to our earthly selves. Instead, "flesh" is shorthand for human powers and abilities, the part of us that desires to live independently of God.[4]

What this definition tells us is that the "self" is not the enemy. Our bodies are not the enemy either. We often blame our bodies for undermining our souls, but the two are not at war. As Dallas Willard put it, "The spiritual and bodily are by no means opposed in human life—they are complementary."[5] The problem is not the body but the *flesh*, the human power that opposes dependence on God. This means God has no interest in making the self disappear. Becoming one with Christ does not mean God is trying to erase us, our bodies, or our souls. In fact, he desires just the opposite. God wants us to be our truest selves, and that is only possible through Christ. C. S. Lewis famously explained it this way:

> There are no real personalities anywhere else. Until you have given up your self to Him you will not have a real self. Sameness is to be found most among the most "natural" men, not among those who surrender to Christ. How monotonously alike all the great tyrants and conquerors have been: how gloriously different are the saints.[6]

With these words, Lewis captures the paradox of self-forgetfulness: by focusing less on ourselves and more on Christ, we become our truest selves.

God's desire is not to diminish us but to resurrect us. He wants us to become the creations he intended all along, dignified, *good*, reflections of him. The image of God in us was marred by the effects of sin, but it is restored to us in Christ every day. The more we become like him, the more we become our truest selves, rather than cheap imitations of others.

Healed for More

This sounds silly now, but when I was younger, I didn't fully understand the value of healing. Whenever I attended women's conferences, I watched women stream down the aisles, sobbing over wounds from their past and declaring their freedom in Christ. I observed all this and shrugged. I couldn't relate to it at all. At that time in my life, I had only a few cuts and bruises, but no big emotional scars. The world had been relatively kind to me, so my healing was a neat and tidy process, and I was eager to move on to other things.

When we look at Jesus and his own priorities, we encounter a very different perspective. Healing was not an interruption or a speed bump on the way to matters more pressing. Instead it consumed a large portion of his time. Jesus delighted to heal people, to listen to their pain, and to weep alongside them. He knew better than anyone that healing is a sign of the kingdom of God, not a lesser priority or a thing to be rushed. Jesus also understood that we cannot "run the race marked out for us" (Heb. 12:1) if we are too wounded even to stand.

Healing mattered to Jesus, which means it matters to us. It's a promise we have in Christ, and it's our mission in the world, but it's also an act of stewardship. Every runner knows that running requires a healthy body. When preparing for a race, you cannot neglect your diet or jog on a broken leg. Your body needs attention and healing and care, and your spiritual life is the same. God commands us to stop and rest so that we can better serve him, our families, our communities, and our friends. That's what makes his race so unique. It's the only race in which rest is a part of the running. We recuperate *so that* we can run.

This race is also unique in that it heals us *as* we run. The more we pursue God, the more whole we become, because running is what we were created for. God designed us for an all-out, arm-pumping, feet-pounding sprint after him. That race is the place you will feel most fully alive, so give yourself time to heal when you need it, and honor God's command to rest, but also remember this: healing doesn't happen on the sidelines alone. We heal to run, and we run to heal.

Focus Verse

"There remains, then, a Sabbath-rest for the people of God; for anyone who enters God's rest also rests from their works, just as God did from his. Let us, therefore, make every effort to enter that rest."—Hebrews 4:9–11

Focus Prayer

Loving Father, I know you love me and care for me, which is why you sent your Son. Your desire for me is healing and restoration, which can only be found in you alone. Help me to see myself through your eyes, and to steward my life with the same tenderness and love as you. Guard my focus from self-absorption, but teach me to honor myself as one who reflects your good and glorious image.

Discussion Questions

1. How has the martyr complex played out in your life or the life of someone you know?
2. If the martyr complex is something you struggle with, what are your personal motives behind it?
3. Have you ever felt like you were battling with yourself? What was the source of the conflict?
4. Our culture is all about being your "true self," but we also become our truest selves in Christ. What are the differences

between a worldly approach to the "true self" and a godly approach?

5. Throughout this book, we have talked about focusing on God instead of ourselves. However, healing is an important step in that process. How can we give attention to ourselves without getting stuck on ourselves?

Epilogue

Too Small a Thing

*I*n Isaiah 49, God says something unexpected. By way of the prophet Isaiah, God foretells the coming Messiah, or "Servant of the Lord," who will one day restore the "tribes of Jacob" and deliver them out of captivity. It was an assurance the Israelites needed and a hope that sustained them, but they wouldn't have expected the words that came after.

In verse 6, God clarifies his intentions for this Servant of the Lord:

> *It is too small a thing for you to be my servant*
>   *to restore the tribes of Jacob*
>   *and bring back those of Israel I have kept.*
> *I will also make you a light for the Gentiles,*
>   *that my salvation may reach to the ends of the earth.*

The term "Gentiles" is shorthand for "everyone else"—everyone outside of Israel—meaning God's plans were far more sweeping than the Israelites ever dreamed. God was broadening the scope of his story to the ends of the earth, essentially saying this:

This story of your journey, your brokenness, your redemption? **This story is not about you.** All this time, you thought the plan was the restoration of Israel—and oh, my children, it is!—but that's only just the beginning of it, because I am interested in far more than Israel. I am going to restore the whole world.

God wasn't rescuing Israel alone. He was rescuing us all. And this would have been surprising news to the Israelites who, as God's people, believed the story was about them. Granted, they weren't entirely wrong. A lot of the story was about them. God had good plans for Israel, but that mission, on its own, was not the whole of the dream. God was after all of creation, and anything less was just too small a thing.

In many ways, this story captures the message of this book. I don't want to detract from the good messages of healing and wholeness in popular Christian teaching. Even so-called "self-help" books can play an important role in the work of the church. God cares about our healing, peace, and joy, which are the firstfruits of our salvation. Eternal life is not a far-off promise, but an in-breaking reality that begins the moment we say yes to Christ. We taste that salvation every day, when we experience freedom and contentment in him.

But if that is all we are after, if that is the end point of our faith, the purpose of our gospel, and what we believe God exists to do, it is too small a thing. God has a plan infinitely bigger than our self-esteem. Our healing is only one piece of the puzzle, so we cannot settle for a gospel that has "personal satisfaction" at its core. It's counterintuitive, but this me-centered gospel cannot give us what we want. It only makes the burden bigger and our faith smaller.

That's why God calls us into a bigger story. And strangely enough, the bigger story will give us the joy we seek. When we stop living for ourselves and live fully focused on God, we will encounter freedom and lightness like never before.

Of course, this is about more than living an abundant life. It's also about the world, which needs the gospel now as much as ever. As wars rage, children are trafficked, families go hungry, and darkness runs wild, the world needs people of courage, conviction, and action. And the enemy knows this, which is why he does everything in his power to keep us out of the mission and focused on ourselves. He paralyzes us with lies and insecurity, and sometimes he even enlists the church into his scheme. As long as he can keep our focus inward, he enjoys a minor victory.

Thankfully, we don't have to choose between fulfillment and self-forgetfulness, or between the abundant life and the obedient one. We can have both in Christ. So I invite you to embrace the freedom of this bigger story. Don't settle for a focus that is partially about Christ but mostly about you. Messages about your worth and your belonging are good, but they are also too small a thing, and you were meant for more.

Acknowledgments

When I look back on this book's journey into existence, one thing is clear (and fitting): it was not about me. This book is not the fruit of my individual labor, but my community. I would not have had the time, the energy, the mental capacity, or the spiritual insight to write these words without the support, encouragement, and sharpening of my people.

At the top of that list is, of course, my family. If this book is any good at all, it's because of my husband, Ike. He is a living theological encyclopedia who also happens to possess the wisdom of a man twice his age. He is knowledge and grace personified, the perfect sounding board for my ideas. He sacrificed time and money to support me in my calling, while leading our family in selflessness and humility. I could write an entire book on all that he has taught me, but suffice it to say, God has shown me his most extravagant love and grace through Ike. Babe, I love you, and I'm so glad you're my running mate for this race.

To my boys, Isaac and Coen, who often served as beautiful instruments of many of the lessons in this book. You both are too young to remember these gritty days of writing, but your legacy in these pages is joy. Every single day, you lightened my spirit and delighted my heart. My love for you is inexhaustible, and I am giddy watching you grow into who God created you to be.

I am forever indebted to my parents—Rich and Debbie Hodde—and my mother-in-law, Ellen Miller. It's an embarrassment of riches, to have so many family members invested in my ministry. You three gave so much of your time and love to watch our boys while I worked and wrote, which not only freed up my time but freed up my mind; I never worry when our kids are with you. Mom, Dad, Ellen, *thank you*. Along those lines, I also want to thank Sandi Barnes, an honorary grandmother who has loved and cared for our boys as if they were her own. Sandi, you have become family to us and a beloved friend to me.

Thank you to my prayer warriors, Marcy Turner, Lauren Miglarese, and Rachel Garrison. Our monthly get-togethers meant more to me than you will ever know. Thank you for listening, supporting, cheering, enduring an endless number of texts, and praying for me and my family. You were the invisible hands lifting my arms for this battle, and I am so grateful for you.

Thank you to Amy Julia Becker, Katherine Willis Pershey, Chris Pappalardo, Steve Daugherty, and Hannah Anderson for your extra sets of eyes, your added insights, your fresh perspectives, and your expertise. This book is stronger because you were so generous with your gifts and time.

Thank you to the *Her.meneutics* community, the OKJFC ladies, and my IF:Table girls, who have provided me with the most incredible friendships. Writing can be a lonely endeavor, but no matter where I lived or wrote, I was never alone because of you. I am also a better person and a better writer thanks to you.

Thank you to Jana Burson, the best agent a girl could ask for. You possess an amazing combination of savvy professional judgment and deep spiritual wisdom. I really do thank God whenever I remember you. Also thank you to Lisa Whittle, a friend and a mentor to me through this process. Thank you for being such an encouraging example of how to write and lead in a way that honors Jesus, and for always being there to listen when I needed it.

Thank you to Rebekah Guzman and Baker Books for believing in this message so wholeheartedly and for investing in me as a writer. Thank you for your enthusiasm, your kindness, and your commitment to honing this message for the good of the church.

And finally, most of all, thanks be to God, whom I have come to think of as the benefactor of this message. During a season of life when I had little time and energy to give, I asked God daily to multiply my offering and grant me my portion of words. And over and over again, he did. He has been faithful every step of the way, the daily bread that brought this book into being. My simplest hope is that this book points people to him.

Notes

Chapter 1 Mirror Girl

1. Christine Caine, IF:Gathering Podcast, 10:31, accessed March 14, 2017, https://soundcloud.com/if_gathering/chris-caine-podcast.

2. Hanna Krasnova, Helena Wenninger, Thomas Widjaja, and Peter Buxmann, "Envy on Facebook: A Hidden Threat to Users' Life Satisfaction?," 11th International Conference on Information Systems, February 27–March 2, 2013, Leipzig, Germany, http://www.ara.cat/2013/01/28/855594433.pdf?hash=b775840d43f9f9 3b7a9031449f809c388f342291.

Chapter 2 Forgetting Myself

1. Rick Warren, *The Purpose-Driven Life: What on Earth Am I Here For?* (Grand Rapids: Zondervan, 2013), 190.

2. Another way of understanding self-forgetfulness is to look at the words "forgetting" and "remembering" in Scripture. The Hebrew word for "remember" is *zakar*, and when God remembers Noah (Gen. 8:1), or his covenant (Gen. 9:15), or us (Ps. 115:12), he does more than simply call those things to mind; he acts toward them in love, grace, and redemption. As author Chad Bird put it in a personal correspondence, "remembering" doesn't mean "rifling through the files in your head until you find that fact you've been searching for." Remembering is an action. Likewise, when God "forgets" (*shakach*) to be gracious (Ps. 77:9), or when the psalmist cries out, "Will you forget me forever?" (Ps. 13:1), it doesn't mean God lost his power of recollection. Instead, forgetting and remembering are about God's orientation toward or away from us.

3. Tim Keller, *The Freedom of Self-Forgetfulness: The Path to True Christian Joy* (Chorley, England: 10Publishing, 2012), Kindle edition.

4. Because the term "self-esteem" tends to be a bit slippery, I want to clarify the definition I am working with, based on a relative consensus among experts. "Self-esteem" here refers to a combination of "worthiness" (i.e., the sense of one's own worth) and "competence" (i.e., how one's sense of worth translates into action). A person with "low" self-esteem does not recognize her worth as given to her by God, and her self-image is not rooted in the dignity of bearing God's image. This misperception, in turn, shapes the way she lives. This definition comes from Christopher J. Mruk, *Self-Esteem Research, Theory, and Practice: Toward a Positive Psychology of Self-Esteem*, 3rd ed. (New York: Spring Publishing, 2006).

5. Jean M. Twenge, *Generation Me: Why Today's Young Americans Are More Confident, Assertive, Entitled—and More Miserable Than Ever Before*, rev. ed. (New York: Atria, 2014), 58.

6. Ibid., 65.

7. Ibid., 66.

8. Ibid., 63.

9. James Meikle, "Growing Number of Girls Suffer Low Self-Esteem, Says Report," *The Guardian*, November 28, 2013, http://www.theguardian.com/society /2013/nov/29/girls-low-self-esteem-rising-girlguiding-report.

10. Anita Gurian, " How to Raise Girls with Healthy Self-Esteem," NYU Child Study Center, accessed March 15, 2017, http://hrsbstaff.ednet.ns.ca/stephem1 /Self-esteem%20-%20girls.htm.

11. Twenge, *Generation Me*, 67–68.

12. Lauren Slater, "The Trouble with Self-Esteem," *New York Times*, February 3, 2002, http://www.nytimes.com/2002/02/03/magazine/the-trouble-with-self -esteem.html.

Chapter 3 When You Make God about You

1. Irenaeus, *A Treatise Against the Heresies*, book 4, chapter 20.

2. Jen Wilkin, *Women of the Word: How to Study the Bible with Both Our Hearts and Our Minds* (Wheaton: Crossway, 2014), 24.

3. Ibid., 26.

4. Rebecca Konyndyk DeYoung, *Vainglory: The Forgotten Vice* (Grand Rapids: Eerdmans, 2014), 20.

5. C. S. Lewis, *The Weight of Glory: And Other Addresses* (New York: Harper-Collins, 1980), 13.

6. Anne Lamott, *Bird by Bird: Instructions on Writing and Life* (New York: First Anchor Books, 1995), 22.

7. John. L. McKenzie, *The Dictionary of the Bible* (New York: Touchstone, 1995), 752.

Chapter 4 When You Make Family about You

1. Rodney R. Clapp, *Families at the Crossroads: Beyond Tradition and Modern Options* (Downers Grove, IL: InterVarsity, 1993), 163.

2. John Piper, *A Godward Life: Seeing the Supremacy of God in All of Life* (Colorado Springs: Multnomah, 1997), 243–45.

3. Clapp, *Families at the Crossroads*, 163.

4. Francis Chan, *You and Me Forever: Marriage in Light of Eternity* (San Francisco: Claire Love Publishing, 2014), Kindle edition.

Chapter 5 When You Make Your Appearance about You

1. Anthony A. Hoekema, *Created in God's Image* (Grand Rapids: Eerdmans, 1986), 111.

2. Shaun Dreisbach, "Shocking Body Image News: 97% of Women Will Be Cruel to Their Bodies Today," *Glamour*, February 2, 2011, http://www.glamour .com/story/shocking-body-image-news-97-percent-of-women-will-be-cruel-to -their-bodies-today.

3. Meredith Bryan, "What Women Really Think About Their Bodies," *SELF*, December 15, 2015, http://www.self.com/trending/body-img/2015/12/what-women -really-thing-about-their-bodies/.

4. "Survey Finds Disordered Eating Behaviors Among Three Out of Four American Women," UNC School of Medicine, April 22, 2008, http://www.med .unc.edu/www/newsarchive/2008/april/survey-finds-disordered-eating-behaviors -among-three-out-of-four-american-women.

5. "The American Society for Aesthetic Plastic Surgery Reports Americans Spent Largest Amount on Cosmetic Surgery Since the Great Recession of 2008," PR Newswire, March 20, 2014, http://www.prnewswire.com/news -releases/the-american-society-for-aesthetic-plastic-surgery-reports-americans -spent-largest-amount-on-cosmetic-surgery-since-the-great-recession-of-2008 -251190991.html.

6. Jess Connelly and Hayley Morgan, *Wild and Free: A Hope-Filled Anthem for the Woman Who Feels She Is Both Too Much and Not Enough* (Grand Rapids: Zondervan, 2016), 229.

7. Abraham Kuyper, "Sphere Sovereignty," Inaugural Address at the Founding of the Free University of Amsterdam, October 20, 1880, in *Abraham Kuyper: A Centennial Reader*, ed. James D. Bratt (Grand Rapids: Eerdmans, 1998), 461.

Chapter 6 When You Make Your Possessions about You

1. Ralph Waldo Emerson, *The Prose Works of Ralph Waldo Emerson* (Boston: Houghton, Mifflin & Co, Boston, 1881), 375.

2. Philip H. Towner, *IVP New Testament Commentary Series: 1–2 Timothy & Titus*, ed. Grant R. Osborne (Downers Grove, IL: InterVarsity, 1994), 71.

3. Anna Jameson, *A Commonplace Book of Thoughts, Memories, and Fancies* (London: Longman, Brown, Green, and Longmans, 1855), 1.

4. Thomas Aquinas, *Summa Theologica*, Prima Secundae Partis, Q. 94, http ://www.newadvent.org/summa/2094.htm.

5. W. Jay Wood, "Three Faces of Greed," *Christianity Today* 49, no. 1 (January 2005): 34.

6. Erich Fromm, *Escape from Freedom* (New York: Henry Holt and Company, 1994), 115.

7. Paul David Tripp, Twitter post, October 18, 2016, https://twitter.com/Paul Tripp/status/788325253672042496.

8. Tim Keller, "Generosity in Scarcity" (sermon), Redeemer Presbyterian Church, November 14, 2016, https://itunes.apple.com/us/podcast/timothy-keller -sermons-podcast/id352660924?mt=2.

9. Teresa Ghilarducci on *The Diane Rehm Show*, "How to Retire with Enough Money," January 7, 2016, http://thedianerehmshow.org/shows/2016-01-07/teresa -ghilarducci-how-to-retire-with-enough-money.

Chapter 7 When You Make Your Friendships about You

1. Ann Voskamp, foreword to *Befriend: Create Belonging in an Age of Judgment, Isolation, and Fear*, by Scott Sauls (Carol Stream, IL: Tyndale, 2016), xiii.

2. Judith Shulevitz, "The Lethality of Loneliness," *New Republic*, May 13, 2013, https://newrepublic.com/article/113176/science-loneliness-how-isolation -can-kill-you.

3. Beth Azar, "A New Stress Paradigm for Women," *Monitor on Psychology* 31, no. 7 (July/August 2000): 42.

4. Lysa TerKeurst, *Uninvited: Living Loved When You Feel Less Than, Left Out, and Lonely* (Nashville: Thomas Nelson, 2016), 112.

Chapter 8 When You Make Your Calling about You

1. Dorothy Sayers, *Creed or Chaos?* (London: Methuen & Co., 1942), 53.

2. Caine, IF:Gathering Podcast.

3. Gordon T. Smith, *Courage and Calling: Embracing Your God-Given Potential* (Downers Grover, IL: InterVarsity, 1999), 185.

4. Tim Keller, *Every Good Endeavor: Connecting Your Work to God's Work* (New York: Penguin Books, 2012), 55.

Chapter 9 When You Make Your Church about You

1. Jared Wilson, *Prodigal Church: A Gentle Manifesto against the Status Quo* (Wheaton: Crossway, 2015), 59.

2. Skye Jethani, *The Divine Commodity: Discovering a Faith Beyond Consumer Christianity* (Grand Rapids: Zondervan, 2009), 125.

3. Ibid., 129.

4. Alex Williams, "Friends of a Certain Age: Why Is It Hard to Make Friends Over 30?," *New York Times*, July 13, 2012, http://www.nytimes.com/2012/07/15 /fashion/the-challenge-of-making-friends-as-an-adult.html.

5. C. S. Lewis, *The Four Loves* (New York: Harcourt Books, 1988), 89.

6. Although I don't use specific quotes, my thoughts here are heavily influenced by Stanley Hauerwas and Charles Pinches, from their book *Christians Among the Virtues: Theological Conversations with Ancient and Modern Ethics* (Notre Dame, IN: University of Notre Dame Press, 1997).

7. Habib Sadeghi and Sherry Sami, "Conscious Uncoupling," *Goop* (blog), March 2014, http://goop.com/conscious-uncoupling-2/.

8. Jennifer Grant, "Marriage in the Age of Conscious Uncoupling," *Her.meneutics* (blog), March 28, 2014, http://www.christianitytoday.com/women/2014/march/marriage-in-age-of-conscious-uncoupling-gwyneth-paltrow.html?paging=off. Emphasis mine.

9. Gary Thomas, *Sacred Marriage: What If God Designed Marriage to Make Us Holy More Than to Make Us Happy?* (Grand Rapids: Zondervan, 2008).

10. Dietrich Bonhoeffer, *Life Together* (Minneapolis: Fortress Press, 2015), 10.

11. Ibid., 12.

Interlude

1. Augustine of Hippo, *City of God*, Book XIV.

2. Dallas Willard, *The Spirit of the Disciplines* (New York: HarperOne, 1999), 172.

Chapter 10 Praise

1. Chan, *You and Me Forever*, Kindle edition.

2. C. S. Lewis, *Reflections on the Psalms* (New York: Harcourt, Brace, 1958), 93.

3. Ibid. Italics in original.

4. Ibid., 94–95.

5. Ibid., 95. Emphasis mine.

6. John Piper, *Desiring God: Meditations of a Christian Hedonist*, rev. ed. (Colorado Springs: Multnomah, 2011), 23.

7. Hannah Anderson, *Humble Roots: How Humility Grounds and Nourishes Your Soul* (Chicago: Moody, 2016), 70.

8. John Stott, *Christian Basics: Beginnings, Belief, and Behavior*, 2nd ed. (Grand Rapids: Baker, 1999), 129.

9. *Pacific Standard* Staff, "The Baader-Meinhof Phenomenon," *Pacific Standard*, July 22, 2013, https://psmag.com/there-s-a-name-for-that-the-baader-meinhof-phenomenon-e5bf3ea87cd2#.t8tnqn1su.

Chapter 11 People

1. "Oprah Talks to Maya Angelou," *O, The Magazine*, December 2000, accessed May 1, 2017, http://www.oprah.com/omagazine/Oprah-Interviews-Maya-Angelou/9.

2. "Bill's Story," Stepping Stones: The Historic Home of Bill and Lois Wilson, accessed April 4, 2017, http://www.steppingstones.org/billsstory.html.

3. Susan Cheever, *My Name Is Bill: Bill Wilson—His Life and the Creation of Alcoholics Anonymous* (New York: Washington Square Press, 2004), 74.

4. Ibid., 91.

5. Susan Cheever, "Susan Cheever on the Real Bill W.," *The Fix*, Jan. 23, 2012, https://www.thefix.com/content/in-search-of-the-real-bill-w8998.

6. Cheever, *My Name Is Bill*, 118.

7. "Estimates of A.A. Groups and Members as of January 1, 2016," Alcoholics Anonymous, http://www.aa.org/assets/en_US/smf-53_en.pdf.

8. Francis Hartigan, *Bill W.: A Biography of Alcoholics Anonymous Cofounder Bill Wilson* (New York: Thomas Dunne Books, 2000), 85.

9. Rick Warren, *The Purpose Driven Life: What On Earth Am I Here For?* (Grand Rapids: Zondervan, 2013), 315.

Chapter 12 Purpose

1. Martin Luther King Jr., "Conquering Self-Centeredness" (sermon), Montgomery, AL, August 11, 1957, http://kingencyclopedia.stanford.edu/encyclopedia/documentsentry/conquering_self_centeredness.1.html.

2. Kelly McGonigal, "How to Make Stress Your Friend," TED Talk, June 2013, https://www.ted.com/talks/kelly_mcgonigal_how_to_make_stress_your_friend.

3. Jen Pollock Michel, *Teach Us to Want: Longing, Ambition, and the Life of Faith* (Downers Grove, IL: InterVarsity, 2014), 23.

4. Ibid., 201.

5. Dave Harvey, *Rescuing Ambition* (Wheaton: Crossway, 2010), 75.

6. Os Guinness, *Rising to the Call* (Nashville: Thomas Nelson, 2003), 3.

Chapter 13 Passion

1. Charles Spurgeon, "The Corn of Wheat Dying to Bring Forth Fruit" (1875), in *Farm Sermons* (London: Alabaster, Passmore, and Sons, 1882), 79.

2. John Piper, "Boasting Only in the Cross" (sermon), Passion's OneDay 2000, May 20, 2000, http://www.desiringgod.org/messages/boasting-only-in-the-cross.

3. Caine, IF:Gathering Podcast.

4. Jonathan Martin, *How to Survive a Shipwreck: Help Is On the Way and Love Is Already Here* (Grand Rapids: Zondervan, 2016), 43.

Chapter 14 Forgetting Yourself without Neglecting Yourself

1. Thomas Merton, *No Man is an Island* (Boston: Shambala, 2005), 66.

2. Keller, *The Freedom of Self-Forgetfulness*, 16.

3. Robert Jones and Bryce Dunford, *I Am More Than Enough: Helping Women Silence Their Inner Critic and Celebrate Their Inner Voice* (Springville, UT: Cedar Fort Inc., 2013), 45.

4. Willard, *The Spirit of the Disciplines*, 54, and John Piper, "The War Within: Flesh vs. Spirit" (sermon), Minneapolis, June 19, 1983, Desiring God, http://www.desiringgod.org/messages/the-war-within-flesh-vs-spirit.

5. Willard, *The Spirit of the Disciplines*, 75.

6. C. S. Lewis, *Mere Christianity* (New York: HarperCollins, 2001), 226.

About the Author

Sharon Hodde Miller is a writer, speaker, pastor's wife, and mom of two. Sharon is passionate about equipping women with the truths of God, and over the years she has written for numerous sites and publications, including *Her.meneutics*, Propel, She Reads Truth, *Christianity Today* magazine, (in)courage, Relevant, The Gospel Project, and Gifted for Leadership, in addition to her personal blog, *SheWorships.com*. Sharon also earned her Master of Divinity at Duke Divinity School and her PhD at Trinity Evangelical Divinity School, where she researched women and calling. Sharon and her family live in North Carolina, where she loves serving the women at her church and in her community.

Connect with
Sharon!

To learn more about Sharon's
writing and speaking, visit

SheWorships.com

SharonHoddeMiller

SHoddeMiller

SharonHMiller

LIKE THIS
BOOK?
Consider sharing it with others!

- Share or mention the book on your social media platforms. Use the hashtag **#FreeOfMe**.

- Write a book review on your blog or on a retailer site.

- Pick up a copy for friends, family, or anyone who you think would enjoy and be challenged by its message.

- Share this message on **FACEBOOK**:
  "I loved #FreeOfMe by @SharonHoddeMiller"

- Share this message on **TWITTER**:
  "I loved #FreeOfMe by @SHoddeMiller"

- Share this message on **INSTAGRAM**:
  "I loved #FreeOfMe by @SharonHMiller"

- Recommend this book for your book club, workplace, class, or church.

- Follow Baker Books on social media and tell us what you like.

  f Facebook.com/ReadBakerBooks

  y @ReadBakerBooks